COMPASSION FOR SOULS

Compassion for Souls

Following Christ's
approach for witnessing to different
kinds of unbeliever

Peter Masters

THE WAKEMAN TRUST, LONDON

COMPASSION FOR SOULS
© Peter Masters
Revised edition of *Biblical Strategies for Witness,* first published 1994
This edition 2020

THE WAKEMAN TRUST
(Wakeman Trust is a UK Registered Charity)

Wakeman Trust UK Registered Office
38 Walcot Square
London SE11 4TZ

Wakeman Trust USA Office
300 Artino Drive
Oberlin, OH 44074-1263
Website: www.wakemantrust.org

ISBN 978 1 913133 09 2

Cover design by Andrew Owen

Printed by Stephens & George, Merthyr Tydfil, UK

Contents

1
Inspiring and Maintaining Personal Witness

THOSE WHO HAVE COMPASSION for souls hear the words of the Lord's great commission ringing in their ears, and long to see the Gospel of redeeming love spread to those around them. This book points to the Gospels and the *Book of Acts* as the greatest source of detailed and practical guidance for a life of witness. (Almost everything in this book is equally applicable to both personal witness and preaching, although the former is primarily in mind.)

Are we aware, for example, that the Lord Jesus Christ employed distinctive strategies for different kinds of unbeliever, and that these may be studied and copied? The Lord distinguished very clearly between people who were indifferent to their spiritual state, and those who were self-righteous, using quite different approaches to each group. It is not difficult to identify these distinctive methods of Gospel presentation in the preaching and witness of both Christ and his apostles. In addition, the Lord regularly employed several 'techniques' for opening the minds of all listeners. Our Lord is not only a perfect Saviour and teacher, but a perfect example to us in all matters, and we must recognise and study the great wisdom of his methods.

Do we know how to stir the minds of both the heedless and the critical intellectuals, as Paul so wonderfully managed to do? Are we able to penetrate people's prejudices, allay their suspicions, and secure their interest, as the Lord and the apostles did?

If readers want twenty-first century novelties and ideas, these pages will be of no help to them, for they are nothing more or less than an attempt to carefully observe the Saviour and his apostles, and to learn from them.

Before proceeding with our examination of these unsurpassed methods, we must consider the biblical commands about personal witness, and some aspects of personal and spiritual preparation. The ministry of personal witness is by any measure the most effective means of spreading the Gospel to multitudes of unsaved people. We certainly believe in the centrality of preaching, which has been especially ordained by God for the regular presentation of the way of salvation. But the chief method for bringing people under the sound of Gospel preaching has usually been the personal witness of individual believers. Indeed, personal witness is often the chief element used by the Holy Spirit in bringing a sinner to salvation. In *Acts 8* we read of a great persecution against the church at Jerusalem, and of how believers were 'scattered abroad' throughout the regions of Judea and Samaria, 'except the apostles'. These believers were not preachers, but before Philip arrived in Samaria to preach, they went everywhere 'evangelising' (the word in the Greek original). From the earliest days of the Church of Jesus Christ believers have obeyed the great commission by personal witness.

This activity, however, is hard, and often risky. It makes us vulnerable to scorn and hostility; it may wreck a career; it may divide a family; it may cost friends. It will often lead to embarrassment and repudiation. It is mostly a 'slow' ministry, involving sometimes months and even years of rebuff before a person responds. And for many Christians it conflicts with deep-seated natural shyness.

No wonder this duty slides out of view so easily, and we prefer to focus our efforts on 'corporate' ministries, such as Sunday School teaching. It is not surprising we would rather devise alternative ways, however elaborate and costly, of attracting in the 'unchurched'.

For personal witness we need constant encouragement and inspiration. These pages are an attempt to stimulate enlightened witness, though much of the material, as we have said, will hopefully be useful to preachers and speakers. A large part of the book looks at the strategies of the Saviour toward unconverted people. Other portions try to show the *real instrumentality* of those who witness and preach, for the sovereign God uses the biblical reasonings and persuasive arguments of his people in the regeneration and conversion of his elect.

We begin with a number of matters that need to be considered if personal witness (and regular evangelistic preaching) is to be enthusiastically and effectively maintained.

1. A matter of conviction

To be kept up with quality, vigour and concern for souls, personal witness must be a matter of *conviction*. The personal-witness-texts must speak to our hearts with all their compelling and commissioning force. No congregation of the Lord's people will ever get down to serious witness unless they are really convinced that God has commanded them to do this work. The hardest duties of the Christian life are only performed diligently when we feel bound to do them by God's command. We cannot imagine a church without worship services, but, to the Lord's mind, a non-witnessing Christian is just as unthinkable. Think of the words of the great commission: 'Go ye therefore, and teach all nations . . .' *(Matthew 28.19-20)*. Were these words of Christ spoken only to the disciples or were they spoken both to them and to their successors in all ages? Clearly the latter, because Christ said, 'And, lo, I am with you alway, even unto the end of the world.' The commission is given to us all to reach out to everyone.

The well-known words of Peter show how the apostles taught the duty of witness: 'But sanctify the Lord God in your hearts: and be ready always to give an answer to every man that asketh you a reason of the hope that is in you with meekness and fear' *(1 Peter 3.15)*. Witness is to be our central and supreme duty, and we are to be ready always to explain the Gospel and give personal testimony, even if the question is asked by a persecutor (this being the context of Peter's words). Paul, in *Colossians 4.5-6*, says much the same. 'Walk in wisdom toward them that are without, redeeming the time. Let your speech be alway with grace, seasoned with salt, that ye may know how ye ought to answer every man.' In *Philippians 2.14-16* he tells us we are to shine as lights in the world, 'holding forth the word of life'. This exhortation is addressed not just to preachers, but to the ordinary church members of Philippi.

Do we obey the Lord in this? Do we attempt to reach unconverted relatives, work colleagues, fellow students, and neighbours? Are we constantly on the watch for opportunities in all our contacts? If not, do we feel no shame, and no compulsion to pray for help?

In recent years we have seen how a loss of conviction has destroyed the Sunday School work of many churches. It is an inescapable fact that the moment believers begin to lose their conviction about the necessity of Sunday Schools, their interest wanes, and Schools fade away. Sunday School work is too arduous to survive unless there is real conviction behind it. The same is true of personal witness. Only when we realise we have been commissioned by the Lord will we honour our calling.

Furthermore, we must bear in mind the great principle taught in

Ephesians 4.16, which is that the growth of a church, both in soul-winning and maturation, depends on the full participation of *all* members. Paul speaks of how 'the whole body fitly joined together and compacted by that which every joint supplieth, according to the effectual working in the measure of every part, maketh increase of the body unto the edifying of itself in love.' If individual members will not witness, the body will not grow.

We need to remind ourselves that on the Day of Pentecost the tongues 'like as of fire' rested on *each disciple*, because everyone was to be a lightbearer. And in *Ephesians 4.11-12* we see Paul stating the ultimate aim of the preaching ministry, which is to perfect the saints for the work of all *their* ministry (this being the literal sense of the passage). Preachers have a responsibility to prepare, train and encourage the whole church family in the great task of witness-bearing. We should not be surprised that in the *Book of Revelation* each local church is symbolised as a lampstand or lightbearer. Every believer is to be a living epistle – 'known and read of all men' *(2 Corinthians 3.2)*.

What about God's anointing on great preachers? Is this not the way in which God throughout history has brought about the greatest spiritual harvests? Is it not through revivals and awakenings that the greatest growth has come? How we would like the Lord to work in such a way that we would never have to toil! Sovereign grace revivals are indeed wonderful seasons of blessing. But where does Scripture say that the Lord will suspend the labour of human instruments during such times? The fact is that in revival God uses personal witness on a massive scale.

In the days when C. H. Spurgeon preached at the Metropolitan Tabernacle, personal witness was far and away the principal means by which outsiders were introduced into the services. Even in revival years this was true. The membership records of the Metropolitan Tabernacle include a summary of the testimony of everyone who applied for membership during the entire Spurgeon ministry, and these summaries show that in the revival year of 1859, the overwhelming majority of people added to the Tabernacle's membership were first invited by a witnessing member at their workplace. Not surprisingly, we find Spurgeon writing to his flock, while recovering from sickness, 'I hope everyone will resolve to bring at least one stranger to hear the Word.' The people were used to hearing such exhortations because it was the constant emphasis of the Tabernacle in those days. We must be biblically convinced that it is the God-given task of all believers to be looking for opportunities to speak of spiritual matters to those around them.

2. A matter of duty and conscience

If we have a conviction that the Bible commands us to witness, a strong sense of duty will add further determination and tenacity.

Alongside conviction we should conscientiously think in terms of duty and conscience, in line with *Romans 12.1*. There are times when a mother in the household feels too exhausted to get the dinner for the family. She is convinced, intellectually, that nourishment is necessary, but that alone will not get the job done. At such times she also needs a sense of duty and conscience. When other emotions fail, these motivate. It *must* be done! It is our *duty* to get up and go to work, and also to keep up our Christian service.

As far as witness is concerned, it is good to regularly ask ourselves, 'What have I done this week? What have I said for the Lord? Have I prayed for opportunities? Have I been a profitable servant or an unprofitable servant?' Perhaps we need to trouble our consciences if we leave off personal witness. Can we be comfortable as non-witnessers?

Conscientiousness is particularly vital for personal witness for the rather obvious reason that it is a form of Christian service for which there is no supervision. A church may organise the Sunday School, the young people's work, the visitation and various other 'corporate' ministries, but there can be no organising of personal witness. The friendly pressure or pace of church life cannot be represented here.

When Paul wrote to the Philippians he told them how much he valued their prayers for him, particularly that he would maintain a good witness during his impending trial and possible execution *(Philippians 1.19-20)*. Above all else he did not want to let the Lord down in the greatest moment of testing. He coveted their prayers that he would be given boldness and Christian character because it was a matter of *conscience* with him that he should not fail the Lord.

Can we not teach ourselves and other believers to feel and to think like this? 'Woe is unto me,' says the apostle, 'if I preach not the gospel!'

3. A matter of desire

The ministry of personal witness should of course be a matter of great *desire*. A longing to make Christ known and to see lost souls saved is needed to overcome our shyness and reserve. Paul tells us that he was prepared to endure all kinds of hardship 'for the elect's sakes, that they may also obtain the salvation which is in Christ Jesus with eternal glory' *(2 Timothy 2.10)*. In his mind's eye he could see future believers living for the Lord, and he reminded himself that the Lord has a people in every place to be rescued from ignorance, folly, sin and pain. The Lord has posted us all to our present situation in life to be a blessing to those who will be saved.

The apostle's way of maintaining desire appears to have been the practice of thoughtfulness and reflection, for he said, 'I have great heaviness and continual sorrow in my heart.' He longed that they would see the Truth, and come to Christ. 'Brethren, my heart's desire and prayer to God for Israel is, that they might be saved' *(Romans 9.2 and 10.1)*.

To surmount the difficulties of personal witness we need the driving force of sympathy and desire. We must *want* to be used by God, and *long* to be a blessing to another soul.

The Saviour was so concerned about people's souls, that he

lamented over the daughters of Jerusalem even as he went to Calvary. Whenever we grow cold to soul-winning we need urgently to pray that the Lord will invigorate and restore within us a great concern for souls. Selfishness and self-concern must be resisted and replaced by sympathy and desire.

4. A matter of prayer

Personal witness is obviously a matter of *prayer,* not only for personal graces such as courage and ability, but also for opportunities. The words of James must apply to witness as much as to other matters: 'Ye have not, because ye ask not.' Even an apostle needed to appeal for prayer that he would open his mouth boldly and speak as he ought to speak. If we find ourselves working in a situation or place where there seems to be very little opportunity to draw alongside other people, then only prayer will bring us face to face with someone who will listen, in that place or elsewhere.

Someone once said to this writer that after three days of praying for an opportunity he suddenly found himself confronted with an unexpected opening for which he was totally unprepared. His shortage of faith and expectation in prayer led to his being completely caught out and tongue-tied, and he discovered that earnest prayer includes readiness to act.

5. A matter of forethought

The need to be ready leads naturally to the observation that effective witness is a matter of *forethought* or preparation. Many Christians seem to think that witness, in order to be genuine, must be entirely spontaneous. We have all heard of ministers who preach according to this policy, producing unstructured, rambling, repetitive and often empty messages. The great proof text for preparation is *1 Peter 3.15:* 'Be ready always to give an answer to every man that asketh you a reason of the hope that is in you.' (*Colossians 4.6* is another.) A planned response is obviously in mind.

How do we intend to open discussion? How shall we answer the various questions which may come up? Do we have any alternative plans ready for those times when we are thrown off track by the common red herrings? Do we have any kind of strategy?

Soon in these pages we make suggestions about the different approaches or 'tactics' which may be adopted. We must never be ashamed to study witness in this way for we are engaged in a battle and we must know and head off the prejudices which block people's minds from receiving the Truth of God.

6. A matter of skill and practice

Personal witness improves greatly as it is augmented by *skill* or craftsmanship. Obviously we are not to become crafty, or to depend upon skill or techniques of argument, but we are to teach every man 'in all wisdom', and to 'walk in wisdom toward them that are without' *(Colossians 1.28 and 4.5).* The word translated *wisdom* has reference to practical skill or acumen. Skill can never win souls, but it enables us to present the facts of the Gospel simply, impressively (in the best sense of that word) and to avoid fruitless digressions and detours being forced upon us by those to whom we witness.

Many people follow hobbies which have become their passion. They read everything written on their pursuit, and bestow money and time to the limit of their capacity, but for believers our all-absorbing passion is acquiring the ability to witness. The writer remembers hearing a group of veteran, inner-city Sunday School teachers talking about their experiences with large and difficult groups of children. These teachers, both men and women, had truly learned the art (and craft) of getting on top of challenging children. With them it seemed to be a matter of honour to know how to win and subdue a turbulent sea of youngsters. Each one had built up a store of anecdotes and approaches which could quell a riot and capture attention.

In the same way there is a 'craft' which can be learned for personal witness. Every believer is *qualified* to witness, and commissioned and appointed by the Lord to do so, but we all need to get on with the task and log in some 'flying hours' to acquire skill and fluency. The sooner we begin the better. Effective witness is definitely a matter of practice, review and tuning of approach.

7. A matter of courage

Witnessing is very frequently a matter of *courage*. Even the apostle Paul, as already noted, though accustomed to all forms of hostility, expressed his need of courage, and asked for prayer that he might speak boldly. How may we bolster our courage for personal witness? Surely, by taking seriously the matters already mentioned. If personal witness is for us a matter of *conviction* and *duty*, and we feel we have no choice in the matter, this in itself helps to overrule our timidity. If in addition we really do pray for great sympathy for the lost, and strong *desire* to win souls, we will be given these things as a driving emotion, silencing inner qualms and hesitation. If, at the same time, we are driven by zeal to take *initiatives*, we shall be less inclined to shiver at the brink, nervously waiting for the perfect opportunity free from risk of embarrassment. And if we *pre-think* our strategy, much of our nervousness will be dispelled, because so much of it stems from the uncertainty of what we should say.

It is worth noting that nervousness is often aggravated because we embark upon witness too suddenly. It is not necessary to launch into nerve-racking encounters without any prior mention of spiritual things. Witness, where possible, should be introduced in a gradual way, and not like plunging into the cold sea. Some people rush straight in, while others do not go in at all. But there is a middle policy of gentle entry. So it is with personal witness. We need not tax our reticence to the limit and place ourselves under unnecessary pressure. We may successfully enter the act of witness one foot at a time, little by little. We may offer people an item of Christian literature as an 'icebreaker', so that they know where we stand and will half expect some further discussion. It is comparatively easy to proceed in this way and it delivers the witnesser from the tensions associated with sudden witness.

Equally we may talk about interesting events or experiences or people connected with our church, not necessarily as an introduction to immediate witness, but as a means of getting people accustomed to where our interests lie, and where we stand. I remember reading the life of Montague Goodman, one of the founders of the CSSM, and of his first job at 19 as an articled clerk to a solicitor. His morning prayer was, 'Lord, make them know that I am a Christian.' The Lord did just that, and in his witness he never looked back.

8. A matter of patience

It must be said that witness requires great *patience* and stickability. Naturally speaking, every new burst of personal witness is likely to run down and fizzle out within a few weeks. We have to prepare ourselves to take up a *lifelong* ministry involving the patient pursuit of every opportunity. It is also a matter of patience in that we should not press people to yield to Christ instantly, by persuading them to repeat a simple profession or prayer. Conversion is a deep work of the Holy Spirit, and we are not to make or force conversions. Our task is to show people their need, to reveal God's remedy, to urge them to seek salvation, and to show them how, but we must always send them to Christ privately and personally, and then pray patiently. We are never to 'clinch' the matter, or put words into their mouths, or assure them that they are converted on the basis of an initial response.

The watchword of witness is – 'In due season we shall reap, if we faint not.' From Moses to Paul, the Bible shows us how God's spokesmen have often waited long for their greatest seasons of ministry and usefulness.

Witness is bound to be hard, and patience particularly needed, because of the stubbornness and resistance of the human heart.

We should also remember that much of our witness has a *negative* purpose. While we have the privilege of gathering in the elect of God and seeing souls won, it is also our task to prepare the ground for the day of judgement, that everyone may be warned and that God may be just when he judges those who would never turn to him.

If we really believe that conversion is the work of the Holy Spirit we shall be prepared to wait for our presentation of the Gospel to be applied to the heart at any time during the hours and days following. When the rich young ruler turned away, the Lord did not detain him with a further cluster of arguments and expostulations. We must allow the Truth to do its work in the heart of the hearer. We do not want to become complacent, or to neglect souls, but we must not intrude upon the Holy Spirit's deep work in the heart. Patience is part of trust.

Patience is especially important when witnessing within one's family circle. Converted young people are apt to rush at the task of witnessing to unconverted parents. They cannot understand why their parents are so resistant and so slow to grasp the Truth. We have heard of how acts of witness have led to family rows, all future witness being blighted. In the family circle witness is unusually hard. It *must* be done, but not bull-at-a-gate style. Remember, time is on our side. Those parents may not seem to be listening, but they probably are, and they are watching also. The lives lived by their offspring will speak in the end and then, perhaps, the words will strike home.

9. A matter of simplicity

Personal witness should obviously never be complex, jargon-ridden or conducted at too great length. The biblical example is to be seen in the messages of the Lord Jesus Christ, which were always striking and graphic. The capacity of unconverted people to understand spiritual matters is limited, yet our natural tendency is to say too much at any one time. If we believe the truth of Paul's words that 'the natural man receiveth not the things of the Spirit of God: for they are foolishness unto him,' then we will not use too many arguments on any one occasion.

Simplicity, however, does not mean being childish. It means avoiding the use of elaborate arguments (often a symptom of our own shyness) and giving clear, unrushed answers to spiritual questions. It also means avoiding rushing from text to text as the Gospel is presented, projecting an almost fanatical and brainwashed image of ourselves to the hearer.

10. A matter of a definite aim

Personal witness certainly involves the adopting of a very *definite aim*, which is that of being used by God to bring men and women to the place of true repentance. Such an aim will make us dissatisfied with giving a few vaguely Christian sentiments. How this may be done is the subject of the following pages.

While we aim at conviction of sin and true repentance, we know that this is very difficult to achieve through personal witness alone. Ideally, witness must go hand in hand with preaching, for this has been designed by God to be more useful than any other form of communication for bringing souls under conviction of sin. It is not the Lord's *exclusive* agency for this work, but it is his *chief* agency, according to the Bible. (The special significance of preaching is emphasised by Paul in *1 Corinthians 1.18-25.*) Generally speaking we may find that our personal witness will consist mostly of the basic need for and truth of the Gospel coupled with personal testimony and invitations to services where there will be a stronger personal challenge. In our day, preaching is relatively powerless to attract unconverted people. It may be said that personal witness brings the unconverted hearers in, while preaching is more used to bring souls under conviction of sin. God has made and moulded these two agencies to fit together in harmonious, soul-winning labour. In order to realise our ultimate aim of bringing people (by the work of the Spirit) to a deep sense of need and to conviction of sin, we need to draw them under the sound of Gospel preaching.

11. A matter of godliness

Last but not least, witness is a matter of *godliness* and *behaviour*. *John 15* is but one of many passages of Scripture which show that obedience to Christ is an essential condition of fruitfulness in this ministry. Our relationship with God must be right, and our conduct toward those around us must be sound. We need to ask ourselves: 'What sort of temperament do I have? Am I diligent in my work, or do I have a poor reputation? Am I a cold person? Do I come across as being vain or pompous? Am I peevish and impatient? How do I react in difficulties? Am I seen as a rather flippant person? And do I take seriously the duties of kindness and good works which are vital marks of one who walks with God? Does my handling of trials show those around that I really do have the help of Almighty God, and access to divine resources?' The self-righteous unbeliever who is diligent and conscientious in his or her job will of course despise the sloppy believer, and disregard all that he or she says about the faith.

The words of *1 Peter 2.11-12* provide an exhortation to witnessing Christians coupled with a promise: 'Dearly beloved, I beseech you as strangers and pilgrims, abstain from fleshly lusts, which war against the soul; having your conversation honest among the Gentiles: that, whereas they speak against you as evildoers, they may by your good works, which they shall behold, glorify God in the day of visitation.'

The godly life, the apostle assures us, will speak to unbelievers. The Holy Spirit will use it. Onlookers will be challenged, and some will be irresistibly drawn to Christ.

Is a godly life sufficient by itself? May I live a good life *instead* of witnessing? Peter leaves us in no doubt that the believers to whom he wrote *were* witnessing, stating that the pagans around them vilified them for their faith. The promise says that a godly life will come to the rescue of the word spoken, so that both would convince and melt those who live in rebellion against the Lord.

2
God Really Does Use Instruments

WE CANNOT go along with those who think that every unconverted person can be persuaded to receive the Gospel. We believe the Bible teaches that all people, by nature, are dead in sin, opposed to God and entirely unwilling to accept the message and challenge of God's Word. They will not repent of their sin or yield to the authority and government of God unless he, by his Holy Spirit, works in their hearts. Conversion is a work of the Spirit, who regenerates carnal hearts, illuminates darkened minds, and inclines rebellious wills so that sinners wake up to their spiritual condition, and come to repentance and faith. If we go about the work of evangelism imagining that the efficiency of our presentation will bring about conversions, then we massively underestimate the lost state of unconverted people.

However, we must not fall into the opposite error, which is that of feeling that there is absolutely nothing we can do to persuade sinners to receive the Gospel. There is a tendency for believers to go to either one extreme or the other.

Nowadays some teachers, in explaining the New Testament teaching on the new birth (regeneration), go much too far. Missing the true sense of historic Calvinism, they say that inner regeneration by the Holy Spirit results instantly in complete conversion, so that the sinner suddenly discovers that he has faith in Christ, and is a Christian. In their desire to give all the credit for salvation to the Holy Spirit, these teachers reduce conversion to an entirely unconscious, passive experience. They insist that when the Spirit regenerates a person, that person is immediately given all the spiritual faculties of a newborn believer, and consequently repents and trusts in Christ *as the result*, or the fruit.

The reader can see that this view removes the seeking-and-finding experience from conversion. Seekers no longer pass through that moment or period during which they feel 'suspended' between being lost and being saved. They no longer come to God as unconverted sinners, applying and longing for conversion. According to these teachers, if people truly desire to repent and trust in Christ, it is because they have been unconsciously converted.

One well-known reformed preacher in the USA describes this view disapprovingly as 'zap' regeneration. All of a sudden you are converted, and the first step of faith is repentance. According to some who teach this view of regeneration, there is no point in trying to remonstrate with lost people, persuading them to come to Christ for salvation. If they have not been regenerated, they will not understand what we are saying, and if they have been, they are already converted. What is the point of appeal, entreaty and persuasion of the kind which Paul and the other apostles practised?

One preacher who takes this 'totally passive' view of regeneration and conversion, tells us that all we can say to unconverted people is that they should listen to preaching in the hope that, as the Truth washes over their uncomprehending minds, God will mysteriously regenerate them, so that they discover they have been converted. We feel bound to warn that such a view of regeneration is not the authentic understanding of the Puritans or of the continental divines, or of any of the preachers of mighty awakenings, and it is destructive of evangelistic witness. But sadly, many believers today have been confused by these ideas. Preachers, for example, influenced by this thinking, have lifted up their voices to say to their hearers, 'Repent and believe, and God will receive you, and transform you,' and found themselves unable to finish their appeal. The thought has occurred to them, 'I cannot say this, because if any listeners feel inclined to repent and believe, it is because they are regenerated and therefore already converted.'

How can the Gospel be preached with persuasive, personal application if we hold this mistaken misunderstanding of God's regenerating act in a soul? And how can any believer witness effectively if ensnared by this view? The correct view, enshrined in the great confessions of faith of the seventeenth century, affirms that God begins the work of conversion in a human soul by imparting life. That is regeneration. But while it is an instantaneous act, it results in (or issues in) the ongoing process of conversion.

Noted reformed theologian Professor Louis Berkhof was careful in his *Systematic Theology* to distinguish between two elements in regeneration, namely 'the beginning of the new life', and the 'bearing or bringing forth' of that life out of hidden depths. Dr William Hendriksen in his *Commentary on Romans* wrote of the 'initial stage' of regeneration which precedes conversion and faith. In other words, life must be implanted first (regeneration) before a person may be moved by the Gospel or understand its full implications. This implanted life will change everything, and the regenerated person will now certainly be persuaded by the Truth, and come to Christ.

Dr Martyn Lloyd-Jones, writing for Christian workers soon after World War II, described the kind of preaching that is produced by those who think unconscious regeneration includes conversion, as a mere 'waving of the Gospel flag'. In other words, there is no persuading in it, no urging, no remonstration and no appeal to repentance and faith. After all, these are considered to be of no value. All the preacher (or witnessing believer) can do is describe the Gospel, not urge it on the hearer.

Initial regeneration may lead to conversion taking place the moment that the Gospel is first heard, or it may give rise to a period of seeking before the regenerated person 'finds'. This is a mystery, as the Lord said it would be. 'The wind bloweth where it listeth, and thou hearest the sound thereof, but canst not tell whence it cometh, and whither it goeth: so is every one that is born of the Spirit' *(John 3.8)*.

The essential point is that the sinner is not necessarily wholly and consciously converted by that initial act of regeneration. The process has begun. The outcome is certainly inevitable, because spiritual life is within. A new attitude to God, new sensitivity and understanding is now possessed. But, consciously speaking, the immediate result of regeneration is to produce a convictable, movable, desiring or troubled seeker. In other words, there is the privilege of real instrumentality for preachers and witnessers. God will use our pleadings to bring regenerated hearts to the foot of Calvary.

The *Baptist Confession of Faith of 1689* (based on the *Westminster Confession*) describes the effects of regeneration with great clarity. It tracks how God calls people by his Word and Spirit out of the state of sin and death:–

> 'He enlightens their minds spiritually and savingly to understand the things of God. He takes away their heart of stone and gives to them a heart of flesh. He renews their wills, and by his almighty power, causes them to desire and pursue that which is good. He effectually draws them to Jesus Christ, yet in such a way that *they come absolutely freely, being made willing by his grace*'[*] [italics ours].

---

[*]   This quotation is from the author's slightly modernised edition of the *Confession*, published by Wakeman Trust. *The Baptist Confession* uses exactly the words of the *Westminster Confession of Faith*. Anyone wishing to consult the Scripture texts

It is the will of God that those who are converted are consciously convicted of their need, and come to desire and long for salvation. They are brought to consciously repent and believe. Conversion is not accomplished in a sudden secret way.

It may be that our words of witness, or our preaching, will be the means used by the Spirit, alongside regeneration, to bring a person to repentance and belief. God uses the arguments of his Word to convince, convict, call and persuade the enlightened soul to yield to him, or as the *Baptist Confession* puts it:

> 'Man is dead in sins and trespasses until quickened [*made alive*] and renewed by the Holy Spirit. By this he is enabled to answer the call, and to embrace the grace offered . . .'

Noted preachers in the past, like George Whitefield and C. H. Spurgeon, saw clearly that regeneration led into conversion. It launched people into a condition in which they heard the appeals of the Gospel with new ears, so that they were moved and convinced, and filled with longing to find Christ, and this was how God chose to work in their souls. He intends that his children should go through the experience of being 'turned round' in heart and attitude. He means them to search and seek. He wants them to be consciously convinced by Gospel reasoning, and to personally, freely and willingly change their minds. To accomplish this, the Lord commissions us to witness and preach to people everywhere. Our message and our witness really counts in the glorious purpose of God. Without the Spirit, we can achieve nothing. But when the Spirit works, he uses our explanations, arguments and appeals.

This is why the Bible is crammed full of texts which say in so many different ways, 'Repent, believe, seek me, and *I will* receive you, bless you, save you.' When a person is initially regenerated, it does not result in automatic and immediate awareness of salvation. It begins

---

on which these statements are based will find them listed in chapter 10 of either the *Baptist* or *Westminster Confessions*.

the process by which the sinner awakens, comes under conviction of sin, repents and believes, and yields to God. Only then does the person receive the awareness of new life and full spiritual faculties of the child of God. Just as in human birth, conception leads to the emergence of a baby after the period of gestation, so regeneration issues in a process which reaches its climax in *conscious* birth.

A great tide of texts throughout the Bible lays down the unassailable order – 'If you will repent and believe, then I, the Lord, will give you salvation.' Regeneration is certainly at the very beginning of everything, but there can be no doubt that sinners do not 'find' the Lord in a conscious way until they have called upon the name of the Lord.

We have considered this point at some length because it is of very great importance. Our zeal for persuading lost souls of their need of salvation must not be undermined by a wrong view of the Spirit's work or the order of salvation.

The duty of persuading and pressing the unconverted to come to Christ is so prominent in the New Testament, it is astonishing that evangelical ministers and people fail to take it up. Among numerous texts affirming this, there is *Acts 18.13*, where the Jews brought this charge against Paul: 'This fellow *persuadeth* men to worship God.' And in *2 Corinthians 5.11* Paul says of himself and his fellow-workers – 'Knowing therefore the terror of the Lord, we *persuade* men.' Let us witness with the conviction of those who believe that God will give instrumentality to all who wrestle with souls in the persuasive presentation of the Gospel.

3
Touching the Raw Nerve

HOW MUCH DOES an unbeliever understand about the existence of God? To what extent is he aware of his sinfulness and need of forgiveness? Must we first find a way of intellectually convincing our secular generation about the being of God, and of the everlasting validity of fixed moral standards? Is it necessary to begin every act of witness with an attempt to prove by rational argument that God is there? Or may we assume that some awareness of God exists, and that people still have a conscience?

1. The directness of Paul's evangelism

One of the most helpful and encouraging passages in this matter is the record of Paul's testimony before Felix and Drusilla recorded in *Acts 24*. Here we see that when Paul preached or witnessed (even to those outside the Jewish tradition) he 'presupposed' that people already knew a great deal, or that they would intuitively recognise the truth of his teaching about God and salvation.

Felix was a corrupt Roman procurator of Judea, while Drusilla, his wife, was a Jewess and a daughter of King Herod Agrippa I. Felix was steeped in Roman paganism. Along with his brother Pallas, he had originally been a slave, but both secured their freedom and rose to high positions in the state. Pallas became a chief minister and favourite of the Emperor Claudius, using his influence to get Felix appointed as procurator. The latter then built a wretched reputation for cruelty and avarice.

Drusilla was the second wife of Felix, having deserted her first husband (the King of Emesa) to marry him. Yet the apostle spoke to this morally abandoned pair on the basis that they could understand their obligations to God. Although Paul had previously given him a 'more perfect knowledge' of the difference between Jews and Christians, Felix remained a man of pagan understanding. Surely, we might think, a series of lessons would be necessary to wean his mind from his religious and cultural background, enabling him to accept the Truth. Paul would have to spend considerable time proving that there was only one holy and just God, by contrast with the multiplicity of pagan gods.

How would it be explained to Felix that so many things in his life were sinful? After all, sensual evil was paraded as a virtue in that society, permeating all art and culture, meeting with approval from leaders and public alike.

The almost astonishing fact is that the apostle went straight to the point and spoke about wickedness, judgement and Gospel matters. Consider the record of Luke in *Acts 24.24-25*:–

> 'And after certain days, when Felix came with his wife Drusilla, which was a Jewess, he sent for Paul, and heard him concerning the faith in Christ. And as he reasoned of righteousness, temperance, and judgment to come, Felix trembled, and answered, Go thy way for this time; when I have a convenient season, I will call for thee.'

The Greek verb translated 'reasoned' means – to 'lay out' or thoroughly present the matter, the issues in this case being 'righteousness, temperance [or self-control], and judgment to come'. It was a direct and challenging address, given on the assumption that Felix would have little difficulty in understanding, and that his conscience could be touched. Felix would not necessarily be moved to deep shame or saving faith, such responses coming only through the irresistible work of the Holy Spirit, but Paul could apparently count on the fact that there would be some answering chord in the heart of his hearer. He was confident that Felix would be able to grasp at some level his condition before God, and that his conscience would be stirred.

Paul 'reasoned of righteousness', or rather the lack of righteousness. Then he moved very specifically to self-control, putting his finger on the master sin of this lascivious and violent ruler. In addition the apostle described the coming day of judgement when the procurator would give account to God for all his sin. The message was unashamedly evangelistic, with no sign of any elaborate apologetic approach, nor any refutation of Roman idols. In this address all alternative philosophies and gods were simply swept aside. Luke emphasises this by recording that Felix listened to Paul, 'concerning the *faith in Christ*'. On this occasion the apostle dealt only with the sinner's desperate need of forgiveness and the converting power of Christ. The effect, in the well-known words of the *Authorised Version*, was that 'Felix trembled'. A direct and undiluted religious message did not bounce off this powerful and hard-hearted Roman, as one could well have expected. Despite the governor's virtually amoral life, and the fact that he had been brought up under an entirely different religious system, Paul's assertions struck home with such penetrating power that he was seized with great fear even at the natural level.

Paul's *modus operandi* has enormous significance for us in an age when society has largely reverted to the unbelief in the true God and the immorality of the first-century Greek and Roman world.

In an environment where people no longer believe that sinful acts are sinful, or that God exists, we are inclined to think that we must *prove* that God is there, and that sin is sin. Paul, however, declared the truth about God, sin and judgement, described the Gospel remedy, pressed the point, and pleaded with people to repent. He only occasionally incorporated a 'rational' or 'apologetic' approach, as though the pagan mind needed deliverance from a mountain of intellectual obstructions before people could understand or believe. He spoke as though people could well understand his message, regardless of whether they had heard such things before.

It is true that many people have already been judicially given over to uncleanness, or hardened by God because of sin, but we must generally assume some capacity to understand. (See *Romans 1.24* and *9.18.*) From Paul's example we learn that our message has unique 'connecting' power, whether people show it or not. If we tried visiting our neighbourhoods and telling people about chemistry or atomic physics, the majority would understand nothing, our words being incomprehensible to them, but when we declare the biblical message everyone instinctively realises, to some extent, its truthfulness, and feels its challenge. They may resist our words, even hate them, and give no hint of being affected, but according to Scripture they will be challenged, and responsible before God for their reaction.

As communicators, Christians are the most privileged people in the world. We are far more powerful than industrialists who advertise their goods at great expense on television. They cannot count on an answering chord deep in the soul of every viewer, which effectively says, 'Yes, I know in my heart that this message applies to me!' Believers who think that every point of the Gospel must be rationally proved before it can have any effect are mistaken. They impose upon themselves a formidable burden of duty, not to mention much discouragement.

Of course, we hasten to affirm that a *deep and saving* response to the Gospel comes solely as the result of the regenerating work of the Spirit. But people are not complete spiritual blockheads. They are *people*, not *beasts*, and they are sufficiently capable of understanding our message to be held accountable by God on the day of judgement for their rejection of it.

2. What do people know about God?

Is Paul's directness of method confirmed by his teaching? May we be entirely sure that a straightforward Gospel approach will achieve a real impact upon the inner sensitivities of present-day, secular hearers? In *Romans 1* and *2* Paul shows how several aspects of our message will be plain and evident to all, partly because they are made obvious by the natural world around them, and partly because they are indelibly impressed on each person's inner awareness. Truths in this 'self-evident' category include the fact that there is one God, that he is invisible, powerful and holy, and that we are sinners destined for judgement. Although people may not yet believe these things, once explained they will carry a powerful ring of truth and considerable authority.

Parts of our message are not evident from nature, nor are they written in men's hearts. These include the way of salvation, the atoning death of Christ, and how people are forgiven, clothed with imputed righteousness, and born again. These truths are revealed exclusively by the Gospel as Paul indicates in *Romans 1.16-17*: 'For I am not ashamed of the gospel of Christ: for it is the power of God unto salvation to every one that believeth; to the Jew first, and also to the Greek. For therein is the righteousness of God revealed.'

However, in all preaching and witness it is a great inspiration and encouragement to realise that the truths mentioned previously are even *naturally* receivable, no matter what class or culture our hearers belong to, and no matter how ignorant they may be, or how influenced by alien religious ideas. Consciousness of sin and guilt may be suppressed by the mind, but it is always there lying just beneath the surface, so that a sermon or act of witness may stir it up.

Paul expresses this very plainly in *Romans 1.18-19*: 'For the wrath of God is revealed from heaven against all ungodliness and unrighteousness of men, who hold *[or rather, who hold down and suppress]* the truth in unrighteousness; because that which may be known of God *[or about God]* is manifest in them; for God hath shewed it unto them.'

Sometimes preachers go too far in explaining what it means for the unconverted to be 'dead in trespasses and sins'. They picture a dead body where there is no life and understanding whatsoever. If this were true of unbelievers they would have no responsibility in the last day for their sin. Being spiritually dead refers to our lost condition before God, but not to the total death of our understanding or our responsibility for sin. Many things may be known about God even with the natural understanding, because these things are instinctual, being buried in our inner consciences and also shown to us by the natural world around us. Unregenerate people do not therefore have to be regarded as totally unreachable and unteachable, as though they were creatures from another planet. Paul writes – 'For the invisible things of him *[God]* from the creation of the world are clearly seen, being understood by the things that are made, even his eternal power and Godhead; so that they are without excuse' *(Romans 1.20)*. Whether Paul is testifying to Felix, who venerated ancestors and emperors as gods, or whether in our own day we are testifying to secularists, the God we proclaim registers in the mind as the only plausible, true God. He may be clearly asserted with only modest sympathetic appeal to sense and reason.

Everyone may grasp, for example, that if there is a God who sustains this world, then he must be invisible because no one possessing divine power is to be seen among the creatures occupying the visible world. The simplest mind or the smallest child can conceive an invisible God looking down upon his creatures.

Also, the very nature of creation tells us something about the character of God for it is so detailed and so marvellous. It breathes infinite wisdom, intelligence and design. It is obvious to people that if there is a Creator God, he must possess amazing intelligence, vast knowledge, and boundless resources of power. Paul asserts that created things demonstrate 'his eternal power and Godhead' so very clearly that unbelievers are completely without excuse for their unbelief. They have no excuse if they choose to reduce their concept of God to something they can make with their own hands. The true God is the most natural and obvious concept to all people.

Equally it is perfectly easy and natural for people to grasp that God is a *personal* God, with a tender heart, because relationships are to be seen everywhere in the created world. Despite the cruelty and heartlessness of human beings we still see numerous instances of love, loyalty and kindness in human relationships, and the animal world reveals a similar phenomenon. Among the most ruthless examples of predatory animals there are countless examples of apparent affection and kindliness towards weak offspring.

It is not difficult for people to accept that the God who made our emotions and instincts knows all about tender love and compassion. He must be a God of great feeling and kindness, and a message about a personal God, full of mercy and readiness to forgive, is a message which every human being should grasp.

Similarly, everyone can understand that the Almighty is a God who creates and sees things in great detail. This is all the more evident in the age of the microscope when we know so much about the astonishing beauty and complexity of things not visible to the naked eye. This impresses upon the mind the capacity of God to mark each individual person, to know all about each one, and to have a close interest in our obedience or disobedience.

The apostle insists that the being and character of God are so obviously reflected in the world around us, that all are inwardly aware that there is an invisible, personal, everlasting, powerful Creator God, to whom praise, gratitude and obedience is owed. Is it possible for these thoughts never to be impressed upon the mind? No, replies Paul, 'They are without excuse: because that, when they knew God, they glorified him not as God, neither were thankful' *(Romans 1.20-21)*. The existence of one supreme God to whom people are accountable is so obvious that if any fail to acknowledge him, there is no possible defence or explanation that can be offered.

3. How the conscience may be stirred

The result of rejection of God is that he is obscured from our thoughts. Paul describes this when he speaks of how people were, 'vain *[or futile]* in their imaginations *[thoughts]*, and their foolish heart was darkened. Professing themselves to be wise, they became fools' *(Romans 1.21-22)*. We become dull and depraved, living as though God did not exist. But our awareness of him has not entirely gone, for it is not far beneath the surface of the mind, and it can be stirred and resuscitated. To do this may produce a reaction of annoyance, resentment and even hatred of God, but awareness can be activated by preaching and witness. The unbeliever may not admit it but a raw nerve is touched when the Gospel is proclaimed to him. He may respond with scornful defiance, 'How can you prove the existence of God?' He may chase down many diversionary alleys, but the Bible says that what may be known about God is obvious to him, and therefore his soul will be challenged. This is a powerful incentive to anyone who preaches or witnesses the Gospel.

How may we be certain that an awareness of God can be stirred up again after many years of vain living? There are two strong and positive statements to this effect in *Romans 1*. The first is in verse 18 where Paul says that unbelievers – 'hold the truth in unrighteousness'. We have already noted that the word *hold* means here to hold down, or hinder or suppress, in this case the evidence of God. It implies that the unbeliever must apply constant pressure to keep the evidence of God suppressed. We must remember that Paul is not only speaking of Jews, who were trained to believe in the one

God, but also of Greeks, with all their cultured idolatry, and others in superstitious darkness. An awareness of God is always present, ready to be stirred into life.

A second affirmation of the suppressed awareness of God in man concludes the first chapter of *Romans*. Here the apostle effectively states that no matter how badly men may have fallen into sin and unbelief, they never lose their susceptibility to the threat of a day of judgement, and this may be provoked. Naming twenty-eight evil deeds *(Romans 1.22-32)*, including idolatry, homosexuality, atheism, fornication, vicious conduct and murder, the apostle says of the evil-doers: 'Who knowing the judgment of God, that they which commit such things are worthy of death, not only do the same, but have pleasure in them that do them.' The evildoer is said to sin against the 'pull' of an instinctual, if suppressed, awareness of accountability to God, and is always capable of being challenged. Paul does not speak of sinners who once knew the judgement of God, but of those who currently know about it. He gives by way of example the sin of homosexuality, assuring us that offenders, in common with all other kinds of sinner, know that there is a coming judgement of God. The homosexual may choose not to retain this in his conscious knowledge, suppressing it out of sight *(Romans 1.28)*, but it is still there ready to be aroused by the message of the Gospel.

Whatever the darkness around us and however ignorant and far away people may seem to be, we may be certain that our hearers can follow when we go directly to the issues of sin and salvation. This will be true no matter how pagan our hearers may be, and regardless of their programming, background or prejudices, for ours is an understandable message, and completely self-authenticating.

Lest there should be any doubt remaining in our minds about whether unbelievers, for all their secular programming, have rousable consciences, the apostle refers (in *Romans 2.1*) to the fact that people possess a keen awareness of right and wrong in their readiness to judge other people. Paul says: 'Therefore thou art inexcusable, O man, whosoever thou art that judgest: for wherein thou judgest another, thou condemnest thyself; for thou that judgest doest the same things.'

It is undeniable that everyone can see the evil in others, and is quick to react when others do things which are offensive, disgusting and wicked.

Paul nowhere tells us that unbelievers cannot understand what we are talking about. He never says that they have not the remotest idea about God, or about his holiness, or about the day of judgement. He does not urge us to embark on lengthy discourses to prove and authenticate the being of God.

4. God's judgement will assume that people knew what they were doing

Paul repeatedly shows that God's judgement will assume that unbelievers knew what they were doing. He describes them as those who are – 'contentious, and do not obey the truth' *(Romans 2.8)*. They are to be punished with 'indignation and wrath' because their actions are carried out deliberately and in the light of clear awareness. This is the case whether the person is an 'enlightened' Jew or a totally pagan Gentile *(Romans 2.9-11)*. Knowing that awareness and sensitivity are present, we are encouraged to step across the very threshold of their hearts to speak the gracious Gospel of our Redeemer.

The strongest possible confirmation of all these things is given by the apostle in *Romans 2.12-15*:

'For as many as have sinned without law *[as given through Moses]* shall also perish without law . . . For when the Gentiles, which have not the law, do by nature *[by instinct]* the things contained in the law, these, having not the law, are a law unto themselves *[the law is shown to have been planted directly in them]*: which shew the work of the law written in their hearts, their conscience also bearing witness, and their thoughts the mean while accusing or else excusing one another.'

When we witness for Christ, we direct our words to minds and hearts which have been the scene of many an inner battle. Even though the conscience may have been bludgeoned into inactivity, it has hidden sensitivity, and may be stirred up again.

Further confirmation of this is seen in Paul's reference to the day, 'when God shall judge the secrets of men' *(Romans 2.16)*. *Secrets* refers to things covered up or concealed. That vital word *secret* is a ringing reminder of the fact that *we know* what we are guilty of, even as unregenerate people. We do not merely have *sins*, we have *secrets*, for we know what we have done, even though resentment of the standards and hatred of shame forces us to hide those sins from view.

All this gives an insight into apostolic preaching, showing their aims as they preached. When they preached of righteousness and judgement, their words stirred up those secrets, bringing them to the surface. Many would have hated and resisted the challenge of such preaching, but within their hearts they knew it to be true.

Those early preachers knew that their message had searching, troubling power even in the absence of true, saving faith, and this was the knowledge that they passed to the next generation of preachers. Note the confident certainty and authority in the words of Paul to Timothy:

> 'I charge thee therefore before God, and the Lord Jesus Christ, who shall judge the quick and the dead at his appearing and his kingdom; preach the word; be instant in season, out of season; reprove, rebuke, exhort with all longsuffering and doctrine' *(2 Timothy 4.1-2)*.

While these words are not to be taken as a licence for a bullying, hectoring style of preaching, they show the Gospel messenger as a person who addresses wilful and responsible rebels who have enough light and awareness to be called to seek mercy and love from the Judge and Saviour of all the earth. These are the people whom we teach, and with whom we remonstrate and plead, and we must do so inspired by the realisation that they may understand what we say, whether they show it or not. Does all this conflict with the apostle's words in *1 Corinthians 2.14*?

> '**But the natural man receiveth not the things of the Spirit of God: for they are foolishness unto him: neither can he know them, because they are spiritually discerned.**'

There is no contradiction, because the 'natural man', lacking a saving work of the Spirit, will refuse and reject the message. It is foolishness to him, not in the sense that he cannot understand it, but in the sense that it is an absurd policy to turn from sin to salvation and righteousness. Surrender to God is madness. Talk of Calvary and the atonement is utterly contrary to his self-seeking mindset, and he will never appreciate it.

It is clear that saving illumination is essential if people are to come under genuine conviction of sin, see their spiritual need in all its true depth, and feelingfully grasp the message of salvation. But even without this vital illumination people's minds may be confronted with their need, and God's kindness in redemption, and they will be held responsible for their response.

If we fail to appreciate these matters, then we will think of people as virtual blocks of stone or as amoral beasts, unable to know anything about God without a campaign of apologetic reasoning. We will take the view that people are too far away for any direct information on the fundamentals of the Gospel. We will attempt to convince them about the existence of God, and worry about our message having intellectual respectability. We will concentrate on evidence for religion, and talk about the reasonableness of our faith. By underestimating the capacity of people to understand, we will become semi-rationalists ourselves.

The quickening of the Spirit awakens mental powers and causes people to reason correctly in the light of what they hear. He gives them a desire and willingness to respond to the Truth and to yield to Christ, which would otherwise seem entirely unattractive to them. He enables them, by his regenerating power, to desire heavenly blessings and to see through the pleasures of sin. All this is absolutely vital to salvation, but even without it, men and women have a measure of understanding and feeling, and must be challenged by the Word. They are still responsible to God, and God will one day judge them in accordance with what they have heard.

Furthermore, when the Holy Spirit illuminates minds and inclines hearts, he still uses the appeals and remonstrations of those who preach and witness the Gospel, and by these very means draws needy souls to personal faith in Christ.

What, then, about the place of apologetics in all this? Is it necessary to convince people's minds, at very great length, about each element of the Truth? The blunt answer is that it is not absolutely necessary. Certainly, a measure of apologetic material may be extremely helpful for various reasons. While it is unnecessary to *prove* the faith to our hearers, an apologetic element in our message may add considerable interest and serve a similar function to that of the parables and other illustrations used by the Lord.

By it we will show sympathy, and appear willing to help them come to terms with some of their vaunted intellectual stumbling-blocks. But really, we know that their problems are rooted in the heart. A proportion of apologetic material may also help to assure our hearers that we are not 'flat earth' obscurantists.

We may see apologetic material as secondary or supplementary means of catching interest, enriching our communication, and dealing sympathetically with the various 'hang-ups' unconverted people may have. But we derive our greatest encouragement and impetus from the fact that unconverted people have a raw nerve which may be touched, and an instinctive awareness of the God to whom they are accountable.

4
Strategies for Different Kinds of Unbeliever

THE LORD JESUS CHRIST and his apostles have provided the perfect example of searching witness, specifically shaped for the disposition of hearers. As we trace the Lord's discourses and encounters, we see certain strategies or approaches occurring repeatedly, and we should recognise their divine genius and employ them. The most striking aspect of these examples is the way in which the Saviour dealt with different *kinds* of unbeliever in very different ways.

If readers are familiar with the classic work of Charles Bridges, *The Christian Ministry,*[*] they will recall that this point is convincingly made in the final chapter of the book. Bridges gives a summary of the pastoral treatment of several different classes of unbeliever,

---

[*] First published in 1849, and now published by The Banner of Truth Trust.

together with selected Scripture passages showing how the Lord dealt appropriately with each one. He lists six classes of unbeliever.

1. *The infidel,* by which he means the person impatient of all moral restraint and scornful of God. Today, we would use the term *atheist.* Bridges speaks of the *sensual* infidel (who is all lust), the *imitative* infidel (most often a younger person who naively accepts atheism with little thought, and then retails its arguments), and the *shrewd* infidel (or the militant, intellectual atheist).

2. *The ignorant and the careless person,* who does not think about the soul and does not seem to worry. He may nominally accept the religious teaching of his upbringing, but it makes no impression on him.

3. *The self-righteous person,* who is entrenched in a system of external religion, but who is without any true personal relationship with God, and without repentance, spiritual desires, or dependence on the grace and mercy of God.

4. *The false professor,* who has intellectually accepted the faith, and joins in worship, but has no personal experience of conversion.

5. The person who experiences *natural and spiritual convictions,* even having a measure of trembling and fear, and yet cannot be induced to seek after salvation.

6. *The backslider,* who is, of course, not strictly an unbeliever, but who may be living as such, and in a very hardened condition.

Charles Bridges points out that Gregory the Great listed thirty-six categories or dispositions of soul (though with 'scant exercise of spiritual discrimination'). Martin Bucer, who wrote extensively on the pastoral case categories in the 1540s, is praised by Bridges for his 'accurate and instructive distinctness'. Other preachers of the past, especially of the Puritan period, have also recognised and classified different classes of the spiritually lost condition.

It is this time-honoured theme which we now pursue, seeking to discern the variation of approach taken to each 'unbeliever category' by the Lord and his disciples. We shall confine ourselves to a study of the four categories:–

1. Ignorant and indifferent people.
2. Self-righteous people.
3. Self-interested people.
4. Convinced atheists.

The Lord constantly pointed to these different kinds of unbeliever in his parables as he described people to themselves. The parable of the two sons *(Matthew 21)* distinguishes between the self-righteous and the repentant rebel. The parables of the wedding feast and the great supper *(Matthew 22* and *Luke 14)* identify the ignorant and indifferent, the self-interested, the militant haters of God, the self-righteous, and the unworthy recipients of grace.

The parables of the talents and the ten pounds *(Matthew 25* and *Luke 19)* identify atheists and the self-interested, and the obedient, while the parable of the two debtors *(Luke 7)* contrasts the self-righteous and the repentant. The parable of the prodigal son and the elder son *(Luke 15)* reveals the self-seeking atheist and the unrepentant self-righteous person, whereas the parable of the sower *(Luke 8)* includes several spiritual states, namely the wayside hearer, the rocky-ground hearer, the thorn-patch hearer and the good-ground hearer. In this parable, as in others, people are invited to see themselves, and consider their standing before the Lord. The wayside hearer is the person who lives on the highway of worldly desires, events, fashions and pleasures. His mind and heart are hard, and the seed bounces off the surface of his understanding. He is firmly closed to the Gospel, representing the indifferent person, and perhaps also the atheist.

The rocky-ground and thorn-patch hearers have real interest, but it does not last. They clearly represent the self-interested class of unbeliever (as we note in a later chapter). Their worldly interests eventually prevail in their lives. The good-ground hearer is the person whose heart is prepared and humbled by the regenerating work of the Spirit to receive the message of redeeming love, and to repent and yield wholly to Christ.

A word of warning must be sounded here. Parables such as these, distinguishing between states of unbelief, must not be deployed in a negative way. Some people fall into this trap, saying, for example, that the wayside hearer is a hopeless case, representing a heart untouched by the Spirit and unable to hear, understand, respond and be saved. But the purpose of the Saviour is not to distinguish between those who will and those who will not be saved. It is to warn people that if they fit into a doomed category, they will not be saved *while in that state*. Perhaps, even as the Lord described these lost categories, the Spirit illuminated the hearts of people and awakened them to see their state, so that by a mighty work of convicting grace they were transferred into the better category of 'good' or repentant ground.

As we describe these different spiritual states to people, whether in witness or in preaching, we long that God will cause them to see themselves, and repent. We are to witness and plead, not to crush or condemn. We stir, provoke, invite and implore people to come to a better attitude, namely, that of belief and seeking after the Lord, and we trust in the mighty power of God to use our words to jolt and to draw needy souls. This is the only fitting approach to Gospel work, and in this spirit we now study the four main categories of unbeliever.

5
The Ignorant and Indifferent Person

W E BEGIN WITH the largest class of unbeliever in our society today, that of ignorant and indifferent people. What approach may we take to those who seem totally unconcerned about their souls? How can we find a way to stir, trouble or interest their minds? Such people tend to be entirely earth-centred in their outlook, hopes and aspirations. Their minds are saturated with matters of home, family, work and colleagues, and with pleasures and pursuits such as films, TV and social media. Some know everything there is to know about the stars of stage and screen, while by contrast, their consciousness of spiritual and eternal matters is zero. Any knowledge they may have about the faith is far too vague to be of any use to the soul.

Unfortunately the ignorance and indifference of this category of unbeliever is reinforced by what they see in the religious scene, a seemingly irrelevant world of waffling clergy, robes, candles, muddle and decline. The best impression of Christians, particularly in the state church, is that of a constituency of strange do-gooders with naive ideas about human affairs. Most do not know exactly what they believe, except that they no longer think that events such as the resurrection really happened, or that hell actually exists.

1. The strategy of dissociation

In trying to witness to ignorant and indifferent unbelievers whose minds have been somewhat poisoned against the Christian Gospel, where shall we begin? Did the Saviour face similar difficulties? Did he have a specific approach for this category of unbeliever? Of course he did. The great majority of ordinary people among the Jews of Palestine in our Lord's time were ignorant of the true message of their own Scriptures, and also completely indifferent. Indeed, they were more indifferent than the Gentiles, because they thought that all Jews automatically enjoyed good standing with God, and this led to staggering complacency. Their disinterest in spiritual matters was buttressed and excused by the blatant hypocrisy of their clergy, the scribes and Pharisees.

We observe that the first step taken by Christ was to drive a wedge between their mistaken ideas about religion, and true faith, and he did this by repudiating the formal, nominal, powerless religion of the day, and discrediting its teachers. As he did so, crowds would be astonished and crane forward to hear what he taught in its place.

The Saviour went about this in a most dramatic way. He would often wait until a tremendous crowd had gathered, and the scribes and Pharisees were close to hand, then, in the hearing of all the people, he would expose their hypocrisy and error. Once, when one of the greatest crowds of all gathered *(Luke 12.1)*, the Lord opened with the provocative statement, 'Beware ye of the leaven of the Pharisees, which is hypocrisy.'

Some of those religious leaders came under conviction (such as those mentioned in *John 12.42*), though most became further inflamed in their hatred for him. But the great crowds woke up to the fact that the Lord brought them something totally different from the cold, formal, ritualistic religion of the scribes and Pharisees. In other words, the Lord employed the *strategy of dissociation* to jolt the minds of the people. He distanced himself from false religion in order to create interest in the distinctive message of repentance and remission of sin that he brought.

Like our Lord, the first thing we have to do is to distinguish between genuine Christianity and the perversion or distortion which most people today hold in contempt.

For many years most unbelievers in the UK received their first view of nominal Christianity from the school assembly and class-room, this usually consisting of theologically liberal ideas. As life went on, they attended the occasional wedding or funeral, or saw non-evangelical ministers speaking on television. They were not impressed. It is therefore vital that we dissociate from dead, formal religion in order to surprise people and open their minds to what is true. Dissociation never fails to surprise people. To point out that many clergy and ministers teach the opposite of what traditional Christians believe is bound to surprise.

In tracking the Saviour's approach to large crowds of indifferent people we cannot help noting that dissociation from error is commonly the first and major strategy, effected as a shock tactic to produce the greatest measure of surprise. In due course we shall add another opening strategy, the use of strong pictures or illustrations.

In the Sermon on the Mount we have one of many examples of the Lord addressing a great crowd of people normally indifferent to spiritual things. Yet he spoke in such a way that they were – 'astonished at his doctrine' *(Matthew 7.28)*. As ever, the Lord made use of the element of surprise, using stunning words to dissociate himself from the religious *status quo*. The sermon opened with the Beatitudes, sentences full of the unexpected. Here was a description of people vastly superior to the religious leaders in spirituality, humility and sincerity. And soon enough the Lord made a statement so surprising that it sent shock waves of amazement and even bewilderment through the crowds. Consider the impact of these words: 'For I say unto you, That except your righteousness shall exceed the righteousness of the scribes and Pharisees, ye shall in no case enter into the kingdom of heaven' *(Matthew 5.20)*. This was a crushing blow to the prevailing teachers, but thousands of people who had long been unimpressed by the sanctimonious insincerity of their religious leaders began to take notice.

What does it do for unbelievers in our society when they see the televised Remembrance Day programme at the Royal Albert Hall, and observe the senior clergy reading Scripture in strange, pompous tones, and 'praying' with their eyes wide open? Such travesties of true religion only seal people in their derisive rejection of the faith. We must imitate the Lord in dissociating ourselves from such nonsense, and tell people that unless a man's Christianity is more *alive* and *spiritual* than that of popes, archbishops, and so on, he will never go to Heaven. Did not the Lord tell the people that most of their professional clergy would never go to Heaven because their religion was not authentic *(Matthew 5.20)*?

Throughout the Sermon on the Mount the scribes and the Pharisees remained an essential 'visual aid', and no act of dissociation could have been more public or more emphatic than the exhortation: 'Take heed that ye do not your alms before men, to be seen of them . . . Therefore when thou doest thine alms, do not sound a trumpet before thee, as the hypocrites do in the synagogues and in the streets, that they may have glory of men. Verily I say unto you, They have their reward' *(Matthew 6.1-2)*.

This was the kind of comment those arrogant religious leaders were obliged to listen to in the presence of great crowds. Repeatedly the Lord placed a great gulf between himself and them, charging them with seeking the admiration of men. Numerous scriptures relate this use of surprise and dissociation in our Saviour's ministry.

The spiritually ignorant and indifferent masses had to realise that his teaching had nothing in common with what they had always imagined was 'standard' religion, and the position is the same today. People imagine that they know what the Christian faith teaches, but what they spurn is only a tragic perversion of it. We long to see people register surprise as we repudiate this, and hear them say, 'Well, what *is* right? What do *you* teach?'

2. Opening the mind: arousing intrigue

The entire method of Christ from the very beginning of the Sermon on the Mount is highly intriguing. The record tells us that 'when he was set, his disciples came unto him: and he . . . taught *them*, saying . . .' *(Matthew 5.1-2).*

Now this provided a remarkable visual lesson in itself, and a great surprise for the watching crowds. The Jews were convinced that they were God's chosen people by virtue of their race, and yet here was something novel and jarring. Christ gathered his small band of special followers around him, and in full view of the crowds began to address *only those disciples,* speaking to them as though they alone were God's children. He did not explicitly state that the rest of the vast crowd were outsiders, only his personal followers being members of the kingdom, but his visual method conveyed this.

He said only the humble would have the kingdom of Heaven, and only those who hungered and thirsted for righteousness would be satisfied. He said only the genuine and sincere would ever see God. He said such people would be persecuted, and told them they were the salt of the earth and the light of the world. How astonished the crowds must have been to hear Christ indicating that the Jews in general were not in God's kingdom, but only the disciples, his personal followers. In their state of surprise, the crowds listened as they had never listened to anyone before.

Then, as the sermon proceeded, the Lord corrected the false teaching of their tradition about, for example, divorce and revenge

(Matthew 5.31-32 and 38-40).

Later in this famous sermon the Lord again distanced himself from the religious leaders, condemning their hypocrisy and showmanship *(Matthew 6.1-5).* Then he created a hearing for positive evangelistic teaching, speaking about genuine prayer, and showing people the tremendous difference between the life which is lived for the here and now, and the life which is lived for God (eg: *Matthew 6.19* – 'Lay not up for yourselves treasures upon earth,' etc). He urged them – 'Seek ye first the kingdom of God, and his righteousness' *(Matthew 6.33).*

Using graphic language (a practice we shall comment on shortly) Christ built on the foundation that the people should not presume themselves to be God's children, by showing that God must be personally sought and found. 'Ask, and it shall be given you; seek, and ye shall find; knock, and it shall be opened unto you' *(Matthew 7.7).* Personal faith, and the seeking-finding concept, is as surprising today as it was then.

The miniature parables of the two gates and the broad and narrow ways divided humanity into those on the road to everlasting life, and those (the great majority) on the road to destruction (verses 13-14). The Lord did not start by condemning their sin, but intrigued them with the 'insiders' and 'outsiders' concept. Those Jewish hearers must have been shaken out of their complacency and presumption by the words, 'Not every one that saith unto me, Lord, Lord, shall enter into the kingdom of heaven; but he that doeth the will of my Father which is in heaven' (verse 21). Then he delivered the parable of the houses built on rock and on sand (verses 24-27), distinguishing between those whose lives were mere outward show, and those whose everlasting souls were secure.

Constantly, here, we see in the Lord's presentation, material to surprise, stir interest, and open the mind. The long-standing opinions of the people were challenged, and their notions of religion confounded. Though warm and compassionate in tone, the Lord's words challenged their standing, and pointed to the need for a distinctive experience of God.

3. Stressing the eternal context of life

A special aspect of the Lord's approach to the ignorant and indifferent was his emphasis on the eternal context of life. This was supremely manifested one day – 'when there were gathered together an innumerable multitude of people, insomuch that they trode one upon another' *(Luke 12.1)*. On this occasion the Lord gave the captivating parable of the rich fool, aimed at jolting the people into realising the empty vanity of a life lived solely for material things.

The entire passage demonstrates the Saviour's use of an unusual and richly graphic illustration to stir the minds of his hearers. People in their thousands would surely have been prised out of their lethargy and indifference as they listened, and their complacency temporarily thrown aside. When confronted by that conspicuously vast multitude the Lord employed *dissociation* as his first point (verses 1-2) and proceeded to talk about the eternal soul for his second (verses 4-5). For his third, he touched upon the fact that Almighty God knew all about them from the hairs of their head, to every word they uttered. The parable of the rich fool laid the axe to the root of spiritual indifference, and repeatedly in this discourse the Lord stressed the eternal context, each point falling as a hammer blow on the hard shell of human complacency. The solemn words – 'And if he shall come in the second watch, or come in the third watch . . .' – warned of the uncertainty of life, and the approaching moment of account *(Luke 12.38)*.

4. Using illustrations

An extraordinary crowd of tax gatherers and notorious sinners listened to the Lord one memorable day when three famous parables of grace were uttered, the lost sheep, the lost coin and the lost son *(Luke 15)*. In these, true religious experience was portrayed as returning to God, or being found and possessed by him. Imagine the effect as wealthy and self-confident people saw themselves described as lost, disadvantaged, purposeless, wasting away and doomed! Yet even in this discourse the Saviour took time to distinguish between his teaching and that of the religious establishment, exposing the proud resentment of the elder son, who would have nothing to do with his father's grace to his brother, and it was obvious to all that the Pharisees were depicted.

In the parable of the rich man and Lazarus *(Luke 16.19-31)*, the Saviour wove his teaching on Heaven and hell into a picture which held the crowd spellbound. Here also was the element of surprise, because Jesus taught that those who were rich and imagined to be so privileged and blessed, faced humiliation and eternal misery. Many of the Jewish religious leaders came into this category.

Such illustrations as the good and the corrupt tree emphasised the need for a radical personal change; a conversion. Any attempt to be 'religious', other than by obeying Christ and receiving a new life, would lead to eternal disaster.

Applying the Lord's methods today

Like the Lord, we must attempt to capture the attention of ignorant and indifferent unbelievers with surprising statements distancing true Christianity from false, and with the Lord's own illustrations. It will only be as false assumptions are swept away that minds will be opened to listen to words which explain the Gospel in terms of a great change, a new life, and a personal, spiritual relationship with God, leading to Heaven.

How may we surprise people today? Here are just a few fairly familiar examples of points which we can profitably make in our regular 'forays' of witness to indifferent unbelievers. It generally comes as a great surprise to the ignorant and indifferent class of person to discover that Christianity was never meant to make the world a better place. The unbeliever, when he thinks of religion at all, is bound to view it through very earthly eyes (as did the Jews of old). He assumes that it is offering something which will benefit people in the way they want to be helped. To be of any value, religion must be able to make their lives happier and more prosperous.

It comes as a surprise to people to be told that the Christian Gospel has no plans to reform earthly society and make rebellious people happier. God has no intention of blessing and improving a world in a state of hostility to him. We appreciate that as Christians we are called to good works, mercy and helpfulness whenever opportunity arises, but that is not the same as secular political and social reform and reformation.

The reaction of an unbeliever on hearing this is to think, 'Then what is God's purpose?' At this point the truth may be stated about the *spiritual* plight of man, and the *spiritual* mission of God to save souls eternally. We can speak of God's remedy for man's rebellion, and the nature and result of genuine conversion to Christ.

Then again, it always comes as a surprise to worldly people to discover, as the old preachers used to say, that Christ was the greatest pessimist ever about the fortunes and future of this world. It surprises people greatly to learn that the Lord had only a message of doom about the overall state and future of mankind. The indifferent person usually imagines that Christianity is smilingly *optimistic* about the future of the world and society. When we tell such people that Christ predicted wars and rumours of wars up to the very last day, a puzzled frown appears, and they often begin to listen.

Further, it frequently astonishes the non-churchgoer to hear that true Christians do not believe that man is good at heart. For some reason people assume that Christians are optimistic about human nature. It greatly surprises them to discover that we regard *them* as being naive about human nature, and that we have the gloomiest possible view about the human heart and character. All these points can be so made that the element of surprise will help to open up the mind of the listener so that we may explain depravity, the Fall, and man's alienation from God. The indifferent unbeliever is very likely to imagine that the Christian faith teaches that good people will get to Heaven (or, increasingly these days, that *all* people will go to Heaven). Naturally we will emphasise the opposite. Because they also think that Christians are 'holier-than-thou' people, it comes as a surprise to them to hear that we define Christians as those who have come to discover that they are hopelessly lost sinners, wholly dependent upon the unfathomable mercy and love of God. The element of surprise enables us to teach the grace of God.

The fact that we believe in judgement, and future punishment also comes as a shock. 'Isn't God a God of love?' the surprised unbeliever asks. With his curiosity aroused, we may explain that God is a God of absolute holiness and justice also, and therefore he must deal with the massive problem of evil, and is pledged to punish sin. Besides, why would a holy and infinitely wise God allow sin to pollute the eternal Heaven? Earth is bad enough, with human selfishness, lies, greed and violence. Sin must be punished, for God's holiness, justice and wisdom all demand it. Even the indifferent unbelievers will listen when we tell them that there are certain things God cannot do. He cannot fail; he cannot sin; and he cannot act in any other way that is contrary to his perfect characteristics. He cannot be unjust.

Another matter which the completely indifferent unbeliever does not expect is the discovery that God does not respond to the prayers of many people. The explanation will nearly always be listened to very carefully. We will have to explain that while God may hear some prayers offered by unbelievers in order to encourage them to seek him, his chief purpose is to save souls, not to support and bless the secular lives of people who have no intention of seeking and finding him. Prayer must first be made for forgiveness and conversion. It will be heard if made sincerely by those who yield to the government of the Lord, and trust in the atoning death of Christ. We can make really valuable points like this once a surprised mind is open and listening.

It certainly surprises and interests many people, negative as it sounds, to discover that Bible-believing Christians are not in favour of the ecumenical movement. This provides a valuable opportunity to explain the key differences between true and false religion.

These approaches provide a route to speak gracious and glorious Gospel Truth to opened minds, as the Lord himself did. We will not stay long with negative material. We will not dissociate from error in protracted detail. But it is an important and valuable component of our Gospel work, whether in personal witness or preaching. May the Spirit of God continually help us to learn from the Lord, our perfect example and teacher, working through us to the blessing of many lost and needy souls in this largest category of all – the ignorant and indifferent unbeliever.

6
The Self-Righteous Person

T HE SELF-RIGHTEOUS category of unconverted people
is second in size to that of the ignorant and indifferent.
Probably, the vast majority of people fall into one of these
two categories. Self-righteousness goes back to the excuses made by
our first parents after their Fall in the Garden of Eden. It has plagued
the human race throughout succeeding history. We observe that the
Saviour dealt with self-righteous people in a characteristic way, and
we may therefore trace a pattern for our own witness.

Self-righteousness is clearly the basis of all 'works' religions,
whether Catholicism or any of the world's non-Christian religions,
all of which rely in some way on the individual's capacity to achieve
moral acceptability. Self-righteousness is also the basis of 'Christian'
theological liberalism which scorns an inspired Bible and the need
for atonement and conversion. It is certainly the basis of all nominal
Christianity, where people vaguely accept the probability that God is

in Heaven, and that Jesus Christ walked on earth, but feel no great need of personal salvation, and may even be offended at the idea.

Self-righteousness is proud and self-confident. The self-righteous person is usually satisfied with himself as he is, and may even possess a sense of being superior to the general run of people. Self-righteous people tend to magnify their attributes and good deeds in their own minds, while minimising, excusing and ignoring their faults.

Before we consider the Saviour's approach to the self-righteous class, we need to understand their way of looking at righteousness, clearly represented in the case of Job's 'comforters'. They believed that Job was suffering punishment because of secret iniquity in his life. Not that they felt that anyone needed to be perfect to be approved of by God. To them, *reasonable* righteousness was enough to satisfy God's standards, and this they proudly imagined they had accomplished. They did not think for a moment that God required perfection from created beings. That was Job's viewpoint, and it had always irritated them. The comforters took the 'schoolmaster' view of God's requirements, one expressing it in heavily sarcastic words: 'Shall mortal man be more just than God? shall a man be more pure than his maker?' *(Job 4.17.)* Their idea was that God is like a school teacher who does not expect his pupils to know as much as he does, and is satisfied if they score 50% in an examination; and awards a distinction if they achieve 75%. This is precisely the view held by salvation-by-works religions, and also by present-day nominal Christians.

Self-righteous people always underestimate the holiness of God and the seriousness of sin. They pull the mighty God down to almost their level, while boosting themselves up to his. To see how the Saviour dealt with this we proceed first to his encounter with Nicodemus, recorded in *John 3.*

Nicodemus would inevitably have shared to a great degree the outlook of his fellow Jewish leaders in trusting in his own righteousness as sufficient to secure his acceptance by God. Yet his mind had been opened to some extent by the miraculous deeds of Christ. It may be that he hoped to recruit the Lord to the service of the religious establishment, but whatever his motives or interest, his mind was at least open to finding out something. We have in this encounter with Nicodemus a reminder of the enormous significance of our conduct and bearing before unconverted people. It may be that even proud, self-righteous people become intrigued and curious about our Christian faith, as they observe our deportment and behaviour.

1. Emphasising spiritual experience

Perhaps the most important element of the Lord's response to the self-righteous Pharisee Nicodemus is the emphasis on *spiritual experience*. Throughout, he presented the experience of new birth, which Nicodemus had never known. It is here that the tender spot of a self-righteous person is most touched, because at this point his spiritual bankruptcy is most obvious. As soon as we mention the experience of receiving new life and new character, following shame and repentance, the person who evaluates everything in terms of his accomplishments is left floundering. The conversation has turned to something which he has never sought and does not possess. Witnessers must draw from their memory store of testimony, both their own, and those of others, or of fragments drawn from Christian biography, to illustrate the point. The new birth is the one phenomenon that the self-righteous person cannot claim to have experienced.

We note, once more, the element of surprise in the Lord's approach, especially in the words – 'Except a man be born again, he cannot see the kingdom of God.' Nicodemus as a religious leader was given no credit at all for his meticulous ceremonial law-keeping. No doubt the Lord's tone was kindly and gracious, but the absolute necessity of a great spiritual crisis was presented as the only way to God.

We also should learn to speak about this great change, so magnificently pictured by the birth of a baby, with all its new faculties. We may show that no one can give rise to his own birth, and that imparting of spiritual life and change is something which only God can do for us.

Christ's encounter with Nicodemus is often viewed as a theological lecture on the work of salvation in a soul. But while it is a priceless analysis of the doctrine, it is also an act of witness and a practical model for witnessing Christians. We must not fail to see the Lord's personal appeal to Nicodemus to repent and seek salvation. The birth illustration in this passage must be seen as a description of conversion. Just as human birth begins with conception and proceeds through the months of gestation before resulting in visible birth, so conversion begins with the implanting of life (regeneration) and proceeds through the awakening of a soul, conviction of sin, repentance and belief, culminating in conscious birth. Following repentance and faith the seeker has conscious possession of new spiritual faculties.

The Saviour did not speak to Nicodemus merely to humble and crush him and leave him in despair, but to alarm his soul and to show him his need of Holy Ghost conversion, and we must do the same. We must speak in the hope that the Spirit of God will work, and that our words will be used by him.

Christ spoke also of the descent from Heaven to earth of the 'Son of man', of how he must be 'lifted up' (as the brazen serpent had been in the wilderness) so that those who trust only in him 'should not perish, but have eternal life'. Then the Lord uttered the magnificent words of the universal tender of the Gospel to all who believe (John 3.16). The key point to remember in this encounter is the emphasis on the necessity of personal conversion, the best way of discomforting and stirring self-righteous people, for they desperately lack true spiritual experience.

2. Making matters personal

As we prepare to speak to those who are self-righteous we may wonder if we will be outmanoeuvred in debate. The Saviour could have defeated anyone in debate, but instead of overpowering his opponents with arguments, he most often kept to one crucial point, developed by apt and moving illustrations. And in the case of self-righteous people, he usually made matters personal, as we see in the encounter with Nicodemus, where the Lord pointedly stated, 'YE must be born again.'

The parable of the Good Samaritan was given during interaction with a wily and self-righteous scholar of the laws of Moses (Luke 10.25-37). The lawyer began by 'tempting' the Lord with the question, 'What shall I do to inherit eternal life?' It may be that he hoped Christ's answer would reveal a departure from orthodoxy. This lawyer would certainly have shared the views of the rest of the religious establishment, and would have trusted in his own righteousness. As the text tells us, his question was not sincere, and he clearly did not think he had anything to learn from the Lord.

These are the usual characteristics of self-righteous people. They do not want to learn anything from witnessing Christians. Some seem to be the most unteachable people in the world. Interestingly, the Lord did not immediately attempt to teach the lawyer anything. He did not launch into a lecture, but 'parried' the lawyer's question with another, asking him, 'What is written in the law? how readest thou?'

The lawyer gave a good reply, saying, 'Thou shalt love the Lord thy God with all thy heart, and with all thy soul, and with all thy strength, and with all thy mind; and thy neighbour as thyself.' But his good reply led him into deeper water, for the Lord responded with words implying that the lawyer had never accomplished this. He said: 'Thou hast answered right: this do, and thou shalt live.' What could the lawyer say to this? As an eminent member of the religious establishment, it had been publicly suggested that he did not love and serve God as he should, and that he had much progress to make. Would he protest, saying, 'But I already do all these things!' thus appearing complacent or conceited, or would he let the rather humiliating implication of Christ's words go unchallenged? There was only one way out of his dilemma, and he took it. He quibbled over words.

Obviously we cannot match the divine expertise of the Lord in producing this kind of position within seconds, but we can learn that our objective should be to make the self-righteous person face up to his position, lay a finger on his soul, and help him to realise that his heart is not right before God.

The lawyer, to escape from the trap and to justify himself, put another question, 'Who is my neighbour?' He then found himself listening to a captivating parable about the hardness and hypocrisy of the human heart, even priests and Levites, and this leads us to the next point to be emphasised in witnessing to self-righteous people.

3. Emphasising the sins of the heart

The parable of the good Samaritan teaches us how to approach those plagued by a self-righteous spirit, and also includes a provocative element calculated to arouse the attention of the listener. Confronted by an audience including many religious leaders, the Lord portrayed the clergy as hard-hearted hypocrites, and selected a Samaritan as hero of the day. This was an obvious use of shock tactics, given the contempt of Jews for Samaritans. By this the Lord again distanced himself from the religious errors of the time in order to teach that true godliness does not spring from ceremonial observance, or outward matters, but from the *heart* and *character* of a person. Thus a Samaritan, regarded by them as unclean, emerged as the one who showed true godliness.

Just as the heartlessness and pride of the self-righteous priestly community was exposed by Christ, so today we must expose the inadequate idea of righteousness which makes the self-righteous person so satisfied with himself. The Jewish leaders focused on *external* conduct such as services, washings, fastings, sacrifices, and details of clothing, all the while ignoring the heart sins, such as pride, selfishness, deceit, greed and lust. We must identify *heart sins* as deep-seated perversions which make everyone guilty, hopeless and offensive to Almighty God. These are the sins to which they are blind. We must tell self-righteous people that God sees the state of our hearts.

We cannot, of course, make direct, personal applications in the course of personal witness, for that would be taken as rude and offensive, but we can speak in general terms of human sin in the sight of God. It is often better to give the hardest challenges by bringing a person under the sound of Gospel preaching, the genius of which is that by addressing many people it avoids personal offence, and yet pinpoints sin. Personal witness can make use of Christ's parables to the self-righteous, speaking in the third person, and so keeping witness courteous without forfeiting clarity.

Our Lord's example with self-righteous people tells us that the ultimate aim of our witness is to show that God judges them not according to how they imagine themselves to be, but according to the real condition of their hearts. How will today's self-righteous people stand on the day of judgement when the secrets of all hearts are revealed? As we have noted, self-righteous people boost themselves up in their own estimation, and pull God down to their level. In imagining that God will be pleased with them, they attribute to God their own superficial standards. They need to see what they are doing. We need to emphasise that it is impossible to know God, due to his infinite holiness and purity, or to go to Heaven without sincere repentance and conversion.

In *Luke 11.37-44* we see how the Lord dealt with a proud Pharisee with whom he went to dine: 'And as he spake, a certain Pharisee besought him to dine with him: and he went in, and sat down to meat. And when the Pharisee saw it, he marvelled that he had not first washed before dinner.'

Of course the Lord did not forget to wash, but omitted the procedure deliberately, even provocatively, and said to his host: 'Now do ye Pharisees make clean the outside of the cup and the platter; but your inward part is full of ravening and wickedness.' The Lord's method is not intended as an exact pattern for us to follow. He was the Lord of Glory and could see into the Pharisee's heart. He possessed perfect knowledge and sovereign authority to be able to speak as he did. We cannot be so blunt so early, especially when a guest in someone's house. Nevertheless, we learn from our Saviour's words what our *objective* should be, even if our procedure is more gradual and gentle. The Lord's aim was to destroy the fabric of the Pharisee's self-satisfaction, which lay in *external* behaviour. The Saviour turned the spotlight on *internal* behaviour; the *heart* sins. Quite often we have the opportunity to make these points in a general and detached manner. When there is a discussion about religion we may be able to develop the theme that the Lord looks upon the heart when he evaluates people. We do not have to make direct accusations or remarks to any self-righteous person. We point out in a dispassionate way that inner appetites, pride, deceit, and so forth are the disfigurations which make us offensive to God, and make us appear 'wretched, and miserable, and poor, and blind, and naked' in his holy sight. This emphasis was certainly that of the Lord, as seen in his words: 'Woe unto you, scribes and Pharisees, hypocrites! for ye are as graves which appear not, and the men that walk over them are not aware of them' (*Luke 11.44*). They looked impressive as they preened themselves in religious finery, but the hearts behind the robes were to God's view full of corruption.

4. Exposing petty niceties

In addition to teaching the contrast between external righteousness and heart sins, there is another distinction which the modern self-righteous person must be shown. He needs to be shown how God distinguishes between *minor* matters and *major* matters, because the modern self-righteous person evaluates his performance in terms of lesser niceties. He is so often concerned with matters of culture and refinement, such as possessing the right social graces. This is certainly not to suggest that good manners are unimportant, but, as we know, they do not count for eternal salvation. The Lord aimed this particular arrow of conviction at the hearts of self-righteous Pharisees in these words: 'Woe unto you, Pharisees! for ye tithe mint and rue and all manner of herbs, and pass over judgment and the love of God' *(Luke 11.42)*.

Self-righteous people today often feel superior even over matters of dress-sense, decor and taste. They are deeply concerned about money, status, and even accents. The list of peripheral and external shibboleths is almost endless, while God requires humility, meekness, love, concern for others, separation from evil, unselfishness and, above all, love, loyalty and obedience to himself and his cause. The self-righteous person knows nothing of these things and must be brought to realise that in God's sight he is a proud, deluded 'externalist'; a fanatic for the trivial, and a neglecter of all truly important values.

5. Exposing contrived 'righteousness' which is just for show

The Lord put his finger on yet another major fault with this class of unbeliever when he said, 'Woe unto you, Pharisees! for ye love the uppermost seats in the synagogues, and greetings in the markets' *(Luke 11.43)*. He showed that even their external works were maintained chiefly to impress those who noticed them. All their imagined righteousness was performed for watching eyes. They were not capable of genuine and sincere decency, righteousness or charity. They were not moved by their consciences, which were virtually dead, but by their love of notice and reputation. Today, self-righteousness puts on its charming, courteous face for the guests, but this changes very quickly once the guests are gone. By way of parallel, how quickly the middle classes of Britain abandoned the external pretence of high moral standards when the 'new morality' of the 1960s appeared, and the old values were no longer generally admired and respected. What was the point of maintaining approval of the Christian moral tradition when no one any longer applauded?

We remember the Lord's words about the Pharisees – 'Take heed that ye do not your alms before men, to be seen of them' *(Matthew 6.1)*. As the Lord said, they sounded a trumpet before they did their righteous deeds, and prayed standing at the corners of the streets. They revealed in their deportment all the symptoms of self-righteousness, with all its love of admiring eyes and reputation. To do the right thing out of a sincere heart, and to live in order to please God, was not their way.

6. Dismantling comparative righteousness

In the parable of the Pharisee and the publican the Saviour exposed the technique by which self-righteous people boost their delusion of moral decency and good nature, and we shall need to expose this also. *Luke 18.9* records how the Lord spoke to 'certain which trusted in themselves that they were righteous, and despised others', telling them the parable of the Pharisee and the publican. This is an ideal parable for weaving into our witness.

The Lord showed how self-righteous people engage in the trick of *comparative righteousness*. They convince themselves of their fine performance and character by comparing themselves, not with good people, but with those who have many obvious faults, and who are moral and social failures. In the parable the Pharisee spotted a tax collector who had committed certain sins which he, the Pharisee, had not committed. Immediately he began to wallow in self-congratulation, while he denigrated the tax collector. All self-righteous people employ this method. They are critical and fault-finding in all kinds of ways. Every disdainful sneer is another rung on the ladder of self-elevation, and Christ's parable is designed to bring them to real self-awareness.

The self-righteous hearers of Christ's day were offended by the outcome of this parable, for the Pharisee stood condemned, while the repentant tax collector emerged as the one who had standing with God. Once again the Lord used the element of the unexpected to surprise listeners, and to impress his lesson upon their minds. Overall, the Lord showed that the prayers of the self-righteous are not heard because they are proud, do not ask for forgiveness, and exclude *heart* sins from their thinking. God particularly hates pride, and will not deal with pompous and haughty people. The personal pronoun 'I' occurs five times in the Pharisee's short prayer, though it is more of a boast than a prayer, and the point is made – God sees through comparative righteousness.

7. Exposing bondage to ego and possessions

The case of the rich young ruler *(Luke 18.18-27)* sheds further light on how to approach the self-righteous. Luke records that 'a certain ruler asked him, saying, Good Master, what shall I do to inherit eternal life?' The Lord first questioned this man about the second table of the law. In reply, he showed his hopelessly superficial view of sin by claiming to have kept all those commandments. Interpreted in the most narrow sense, it is possible that he had kept them, but the problem with self-righteous people is that standards are always interpreted in the narrowest possible way. The young man may have been innocent of physical adultery, but what about lust? He had not killed, but was he guilty of hatred, rage, malice or unkindness? He had not actually stolen, but what of extortion, taking advantage, underpaying his employees, and so on? He had not falsely charged anyone with a crime, but what about lies, excuses, slander and back-biting? As Bishop Ryle says of this young man, 'An answer more full of darkness and self-ignorance it is impossible to conceive! He who made it could have known nothing rightly, either about himself, or God, or God's law.' Such is the condition of all self-righteous people.

The Lord's main challenge came when he put his finger on the young ruler's greatest defect and sin, his bondage to the dictates of ego, and to his possessions. His twin gods were his exalted position in society, and his riches. When the Saviour invited him to sell everything he possessed and follow him, the young man could not do it. He would have followed Christ, in his own way, only if it had been possible for him to keep his shrine and idols – his ego and possessions.

If only we could show self-righteous people their bondage! If only we could prick that balloon of complacent superiority and self-satisfaction! And to some extent we can, by using this searching account in our explanation of true conversion. Here is a picture of people who will not yield to Christ because they are held in the clutches of pride and service of self, and cannot break the hold of these sins. Patiently but clearly we must convey this to self-righteous people. Their lives bring nothing at all to the true God, but they are the poor slaves of two gods – their own egos, and the material world.

8. Exposing hatred of repentance

The final ingredient of our message to the self-righteous is the most difficult, and we may well consider this matter best left to the preacher. *Matthew 21.33-44* records the vineyard parable which speaks of a householder who 'planted a vineyard, and hedged it round about, and digged a winepress in it, and built a tower, and let it out to husbandmen, and went into a far country.' The husbandmen, or tenant farmers, decided to seize the vineyard for themselves, and to beat, stone and kill the various messengers who were sent to collect the owner's dues. When at last the owner sent his son, 'they said among themselves, This is the heir; come, let us kill him, and let us seize on his inheritance.' And they slew the son.

The lord of the vineyard destroyed the wicked husbandmen

and let his vineyard out to others, and the Saviour concluded the parable with these solemn words: 'Did ye never read in the scriptures, The stone which the builders rejected, the same is become the head of the corner: this is the Lord's doing, and it is marvellous in our eyes? Therefore say I unto you, The kingdom of God shall be taken from you, and given to a nation bringing forth the fruits thereof.' It is recorded that 'when the chief priests and Pharisees had heard his parables, they perceived that he spake of them.' This parable was plainly directed against the self-righteous leaders of the Jewish people, and its purpose is to present God's analysis of self-righteousness.

Righteousness is described in terms of a vineyard – the vineyard of righteousness – which is God's property and territory, but the self-righteous have seized it and occupied it. They have no right to be there and they pay no dues to God. They are not legitimate occupants, and worse, they reject all God's overtures to them to inaugurate a right relationship. Even though God sends his Son to make it possible for them to live in the vineyard of righteousness, they say – 'Let us take him and kill him.'

They are squatters in God's territory, wanting to be seen as upright people, but rejecting the terms. They will not occupy the vineyard on the basis of repentance and grace, and they hate and harm anyone who poses a threat to their occupation. The self-righteous person is shown by this parable that if he maintains his pretence and rejects the message of a forgiving Saviour, then he will eventually be dealt with as a trespasser who has seized and stolen a territory. It is significant that in this parable the Lord indicates that the intruder knows what he is doing when he wilfully spurns the message of mercy and grace.

The theme of our message to the self-righteous must therefore be: 'No repentance – no conversion. No repentance – no Heaven and no hope. No repentance means no escape from the day when rebels must stand condemned before the Judge of all the earth.'

The Lord declared to Chorazin and Bethsaida that they would fare worse than Tyre and Sidon in the day of judgement. The middle-class cities of that religious nation were stripped of all their imagined righteousness by the Lord. What was wrong with Chorazin and Bethsaida? What was wrong with Capernaum? They avoided repentance. They told themselves that they were righteous already, and did not need to repent.

7
The Self-Interested Person

THERE IS A CLASS of unbeliever that needs particular care in modern times, because it appears to be easy to reach, comes to faith quickly, and supplies numerous new members to the churches of Christ, but the outcome spells disappointment and disaster. Converts from this category frequently fall back into the world fairly soon, or remain longer to give untold trouble to the churches of Christ. This is the 'self-interested' category of unbeliever.

People in this category may appear to be humble, self-effacing people, not at all like the self-righteous, proud Pharisees, or the general run of ignorant and indifferent people. Their openness and teachability appeals to us, and we naturally form high expectations that they will find the Lord. We do not detect, at first, that they are only interested in our religious message because they have seen something which they like or want for themselves. It may be they want companionship in the church, or something else other than pardon and reconciliation with God, whether they realise it or not.

1. Emphasising real conviction and repentance

During his earthly ministry the Lord Jesus took pains to rebuff with solemn warnings all who tried to follow him in a superficial way, without having first understood the way of true repentance and the cost of discipleship. Several passages in the Gospels show how Christ dealt with this type of hearer, and we must learn from his example. Vast numbers of truly converted people first came to church out of self-interest. Today, they bless God that those who witnessed to them and befriended them patiently stressed the issues of repentance and conversion. There is hope for the self-interested person, because the Holy Spirit can change the leopard's spots. But we must be faithful, or people with only a meaningless, superficial profession of faith will join the churches out of self-interest.

The self-interested class of unbeliever is on the increase at the present time, judging from the success of modern church-growth techniques which focus on giving people what they want. Strategies which shamelessly mix a morsel of Gospel Truth with an abundance of entertainment, worldliness, companionship and pleasure are attracting outsiders into churches and house groups, indicating the continuing presence of a huge 'market' of self-interested people.

In the parable of the sower this class is portrayed by the thin film of fertile soil which covers an outcrop of rock. In this soil the seed is likely to spring up readily, but the root of the matter will not be there. In times of decadence, when conversions are less frequent, even the most careful Gospel workers are vulnerable to being over-impressed by people who make a ready response to their testimony. An immediate positive response is so unusual that we are easily carried away, but what if people have only become interested in our message for some perceived earthly and personal benefit, such as companionship, or intellectual explanations of their existence? What if they accept all we tell them, learn the language of Zion, and join the local church, to be a thorn in our side for years to come? It has often been said that most of the difficulties which churches experience are due to the presence of unconverted people in their membership. Pastors complain of members who grumble, grimace and show no enthusiasm for spiritual things, but who just inflame any and every difficulty which comes along.

In the past, mass evangelistic crusades were probably the main culprits for canvassing and enlisting self-interested people, then rushing them into making professions before they had time to think what they were doing. We do not say that mass evangelism is intrinsically wrong, but in modern times it has usually featured a shallow Gospel presentation, coupled with a goal of producing numerous instant converts. With the demise of mass crusades, seeker-sensitive churches took over the work of fishing self-seeking people into church without true repentance. Such churches are a wonder of facilities for recreation and pleasure: everything to attract the self-seeking heart. But those very methods have been adopted by numerous traditional churches, that adapt themselves to be attractive to the unsaved heart, seldom mentioning sin and repentance.

2. Avoiding earthly incentives

The longest chapter of *John's Gospel* (having 71 verses) is devoted to showing how the Lord dealt with people who followed him for the wrong reasons. *John 6.2* sets the scene: 'And a great multitude followed him, because they saw his miracles which he did on them that were diseased.' This crowd flocked after the Lord, always ready to listen and to go to great lengths to track him down. Yet the chapter shows that most of them, in the end, had no interest in his spiritual message, nor any inclination to repent of their sin. They saw other things which interested them.

Some of them wanted to see spectacular healing miracles. Others wanted to see the Lord assume power as a national leader, fulfilling no doubt the Jewish longing for someone who would rid them of the Roman army of occupation, and revitalise their national fortunes *(John 6.15)*. They wanted exciting events to enter into their dreary lives. Not having televisions, cinemas, nor all the other things that worldlings depend upon today, they looked to the great orator and miracle-worker as the most exciting prospect in Israel for many generations.

The Lord, however, did not encourage unenlightened enthusiasm, as so many do today, such as the charismatics who use healing and prosperity as bait to attract adherents. The Lord faced people with their true motives, and if they made no progress in a spiritual direction, he actually put them off. By the end of *John 6*, we read that, 'Many of his disciples went back, and walked no more with him' (verse 66). This was the result of our Lord's warnings to them. When faced with superficial interest, he put it to the test and questioned it. He made the terms of discipleship so clear that only people with a real spiritual concern for repentance and life continued to follow him.

3. True faith is more than intellectual enthusiasm

Self-interested folk may at first possess a strong degree of seemingly genuine belief in the things of God, yet fall far short of evangelical repentance and obedience. *John 6.14* records: 'Then those men, when they had seen the miracle that Jesus did, said, This is of a truth that prophet that should come into the world.' They believed the prophecies about a coming Messiah, and accepted that the Lord's miracles were accomplished by divine power.

Equally, people today may mentally accept the message and be open to our every word in private witness, but may resemble those of Christ's day, who after a while, 'walked no more with him'.

Some years ago an exceptional speaker and writer in the field of Christian apologetic reasoning gained a considerable following in the universities of America and Europe. By skill and strength of argument he attracted large numbers of students and other young people to the Christian faith, but time led to disappointment when most 'converts' slipped away from the faith soon after leaving the university environment. A solidly reformed and powerful contender for the Gospel and for a Christian worldview saw his following peak and fade, but why? The answer is that this demonstration of powerful apologetic evangelism happened to coincide with a period during which students had become disenchanted with materialistic philosophy, with its weak explanation of the phenomena of life and human behaviour, and its message of ultimate purposelessness. They leapt at something intellectually stimulating with which to challenge the self-seeking, materialistic society around them. They wanted some explanation for the state of society, and they found it, along with immense intellectual satisfaction, in the Christian worldview. Tragically, it would appear that most did not experience conviction of sin, sincere repentance and the new birth, although all these were offered. They looked only for what was impressive and fresh for their minds. They were in the 'self-interested' class; the thin layer of soil lying on rocky ground. They were those who, for a time, believed the message, though not for the right reasons, and soon fell away. What does the hearer of the Gospel want? Is it something for the mind only? Or is it something for the heart only, such as companionship and friendship and love (the bait of the seeker-friendly and 'missional' models of church life)?

4. The folly of 'need-based' evangelism

John 6.24 warns us that false discipleship can also be accompanied by apparent zeal, effort and sacrifice: 'When the people therefore saw that Jesus was not there, neither his disciples, they also took shipping, and came to Capernaum, seeking for Jesus.' But the Lord told them that they sought him because they had received a good meal. They had not even been *rightly* impressed by the miracle! Their response was not like that of Simon Peter who, when he witnessed a great miracle, fell on his knees and said, 'Depart from me; for I am a sinful man, O Lord.'

In the course of our witness we may be over-impressed by someone who goes to some lengths to meet us for spiritual conversation, or to attend church. We experience so many disappointments and broken promises that any concerned hearer appears to be different. But such a person may still turn out to be self-interested, and we must therefore keep the basic message of 'repentance and remission of sins' well to the fore.

Nowadays we find evangelists and pastors who pander to self-interest to secure attention. We hear of 'need-based' evangelism, which offers happiness to the sad, companionship to the lonely, counselling and restoration to those in marital difficulties, recreation to the bored, and so on. But if we bait and lure people by offering whatever it may be that they desire, we must not be surprised to discover, in the end, that our 'converts' are sadly deluded, self-interested people. This may seem very negative and depressing to contemplate, but we must always be ready to recognise when there is no meaningful desire for repentance and spiritual experience in a person.

For the self-interested, we must follow the example of *John 6* and make it plain that we bring a message of spiritual conversion. It was when the Lord stressed the *spiritual* purpose of his coming that they began to murmur and question everything he said.

The Lord warned: 'Labour not for the meat which perisheth, but for that meat which endureth unto everlasting life, which the Son of man shall give unto you' *(John 6.27)*. Following this, we read of the deepening perplexity of the crowd, as their minds struggled with, and refused, the message of atonement and the need for *spiritual* life. 'This is the work of God,' said Christ, 'that ye believe on him whom he hath sent.' Belief, as opposed to works, was stressed; a humbling message which called attention to people's spiritual bankruptcy, inadequacy, sinfulness and failure.

5. Stressing the new life and the lordship of Christ

The self-interested person wants something in this life, but our message emphasises an emergency situation of spiritual and eternal loss, unless all our interests in this life are renounced in favour of Christ and the gift of salvation. If the normal conversation of an interested person is about earthly things, we will be on our guard. If there are no doubts and fears, and no spiritual problems (only intellectual ones), then we will be cautious.

Other passages show how the Saviour cautioned people who were self-confident and self-interested. We think of two of the men whose approach to him is recorded in *Luke 9.57-62*. These possessed an apparent interest in Christ's teaching and works, and pressed themselves upon him, saying, 'Lord, I will follow thee,' but it was clear to the Lord that they did not grasp what they were doing, and were full of self-interest. He therefore confronted them with the cost of discipleship. He told them that they must live by faith and cut their former ties.

We, too, must make clear that our message is one of conversion, which involves dying to self and to the old life, and living entirely for Christ. No longer is the convert preoccupied with his future, his interests, his career, his earthly happiness, his security, and so on. He now lives for the Lord and his cause. This was in the mind of the Lord when he said, 'So likewise, whosoever he be of you that forsaketh not all that he hath, he cannot be my disciple' *(Luke 14.33)*. The Lord does not want us to rush people into making quick professions of faith.

When Jacob returned home, terrified of meeting Esau, he prayed earnestly for God to deliver him. But the Lord acted as though to say, 'This time, Jacob, you must really mean it.' And so God withstood Jacob, wrestling with him, so that he struggled and laboured in earnest prayer before receiving the blessing. In a way, this is just what God requires of the self-interested seeker. He must be told, kindly but firmly, that there is no hope of conversion until the Lord is approached for the right reasons, on the right terms, and with genuine repentance and yielding to Christ's lordship.

In this connection we must be careful in our churches of the 'YPF syndrome'. Many fellowships enjoy the presence of a dedicated and energetic youth leader who is able to gather a group of teenagers into regular meetings, often including regular recreational activities. The trouble is that those who lead the work, well motivated though they may be, frequently overlook the self-interest in the human heart. It is an observable fact that often the majority of the members of such a teenage group will profess Christ, and yet may have 'rebelled' or fallen away before they reach their twenties. The passing of years will show that only a few maintained a good stand.

The reason for the poor record of some youth groups is that the young will readily accept the religious message of a community which provides companionship, enjoyment and security. These things are of great importance to the young, and they will be strongly inclined to identify with and profess all that the group stands for, partly to please, and partly to secure full acceptance. They may not be conscious of these motives, but they will be there. Young people will even manifest some form of emotional experience as they accept the message, and in the short term this may be hard to distinguish from true conversion. If only there were less recreation, and more of the spiritual message in such groups, the problem of spurious professions might be more avoidable. If only the leaders would concentrate less energy on the same few youngsters, and more on reaching a larger number, the peer-group danger might be less significant. If only the young people were encouraged to attend regular Gospel ministry with the main congregation, the problem might also be less acute.

A greater awareness of the self-interest which lurks in the heads of many unconverted people, young and old, would deliver us from many snares in our Gospel work. In personal witness, this class of unbeliever needs to hear emphasised the self-renouncing and spiritual aspects of true conversion. This was the example set by the Great Physician. It is only as we stick firmly to our emphasis on repentance, turning away from the world, and yielding to the lordship of Christ, that we shall minister true blessing to those inclined to act under the sway of human self-interest.

8
The Convinced Atheist

W E LIVE IN DAYS of unbelief when militant atheism
has given rise to vast numbers of convinced atheists. The older writers dubbed this class of unbeliever
'proud infidels', a term which drew attention to the atheist's feeling
of superiority at having rejected God. Charles Bridges distinguished
between the *sensual infidel,* the *imitative infidel,* and the *shrewd
infidel.* The sensual atheist rejects God out of lust, for his 'god is his
belly', and he hates the idea that he is observed by a holy God.

The imitative atheist goes along with the God-rejecting crowd
because it is the fashionable thing to do, and because he will not
think for himself. In the case of the shrewd atheist, says Bridges, 'we
find the love of sin gathering strength from the pride of reasoning.'

Atheists are not to be confused with ignorant and indifferent
people who may vaguely believe in the existence of God, even
though they give it no further thought. Atheists are those who have

thought about the matter and have decided to expel the recognition of God from their minds altogether. They will argue the point, and many welcome every opportunity to do so.

1. Avoiding mere intellectual argument

The root cause of atheism is expressed by the Lord in *John 3.19-20*: 'And this is the condemnation, that light is come into the world, and men loved darkness rather than light, because their deeds were evil. For every one that doeth evil hateth the light, neither cometh to the light, lest his deeds should be reproved.' Three crucial facts are taught in these words. The first is that *sin is the basis of atheism.* The second is that *fear of reproof* leads people to avoid the mention of God. They cannot stand the pangs of reproof or conscience. The third is that *proud independence hates light,* that is, instruction and guidance from outside one's self.

Love of sin, then, is the prime motive for adopting atheistic views. People reject the existence of God because they want to indulge in sin and be free to do what they like. The atheist gains, so he thinks, tremendous liberation the moment he repudiates the restraints of a God-ordained moral system. He wants to be morally free to follow the dictates of his heart, his ambitions, his opinions and his whims. He may well adopt some cultural refinements and a moral system of his own if it suits his purpose, but all his intellectual objections to God are produced from a mind acting under orders from the heart, where lusts reign.

The second fact taught in Christ's words is that the atheist has come to his position because he hates the pangs of conscience. He positions himself as far away as he can from God-given standards because he cannot bear a single stab of shame, accusation or aware-ness of his fallen ways. One of the chief purposes of his atheism is to protect himself from anything of the kind.

The third fact taught by the Lord about the atheist is that he is proud, and does not want to be dependent upon God for anything.

He does not want to feel indebted to God for life, health, gifts or provisions, nor does he want to obey him in anything. He likes to think that he is entirely self-sufficient and capable. The idea of being a dependent being offends his ego. He must be the master of his life; the captain of his ship. Under no circumstances will he be a mere servant of God.

These three factors are all matters of the *heart* rather than of the *head,* and while the atheist must have his intellectual unbelief challenged, his real problem is a moral one, namely, rebellion. We will therefore be doing the worst thing if we flatter an atheist's intellectual objections, treating them as reasonable, and entering into overlong discussions on apologetic themes.

2. Exposing the folly and consequences of sin

We need to approach convinced atheists as the Lord did, taking account of his analysis of their unbelief. As they love sin, and value above all else their liberty to please themselves and do what they like, we may emphasise the suffering that results from such an outlook.

This approach is also appropriate for another part of Christ's analysis, namely, the pride and independence of atheists. They partly reject God because they pride themselves that they are self-sufficient. They must believe in the inevitable rise and progress of the human race, and the lofty power of the human mind. The exposing of the ravages of sin in the world effectively ridicules and rebukes the absurdities of such a view, and also the foolishness of the love of sin. When proud atheism gripped the minds of leading thinkers in the 1930s, several famous examples (such as C. M. Joad) were jarred out of their view by World War II and its inhumanity. Their trust in the essential goodness of man lay in shattered ruins in the light of cruel reality.

Today a new generation imagines people are essentially good and trustworthy, and they hate what they call the 'nanny society'. They think society will work without religious moral restraints, but we will speak about the miserable failure of the human race, and about its wars, cruelties and unkindness. The hopeless plight of mankind hits the atheist very hard, because it shouts from the rooftops the depravity of the human heart. We should stress the fact that people are impotent to improve themselves or to conquer their problems while in their state of rebellion against God, and his moral system.

The disorder which prevails at personal, family, national and international levels cries out against the atheist's theory that people have power to make progress and order their affairs aright. Humanity's problems are a great blow to the pride of the atheist.

Isaiah 5 is a magnificent example of *moral* reasoning with atheists. Here God, through the prophet, remonstrates with the Jews for whom he had done everything possible, and to whom he had given great privileges. But they (picturing the whole human race) brought forth wild grapes, the misery and oppression of a godless society. The great 'woes' of the Lord are here pronounced against greed, pride, love of power, drunkenness, pleasure-lust, wilful ignorance of divine and profound issues, reversal and perversion of sacred moral values, pursuit of personal gain, and other 'liberties' of atheism. The burden or judgement of *Isaiah 5* is to show the unmistakable outcome for all societies characterised by this behaviour.

3. Using personal testimony

Because the atheist is running away from the voice of conscience (the second part of the Lord's analysis of atheism), we must aim at stirring it into life. The use of personal testimony is often effective in achieving this as we see from the provision which Christ made for maintaining a witness to an 'atheistic' community on the eastern shore of Galilee. When the Lord cast out the demons from the possessed man of Gadara, they entered a herd of swine which immediately ran down a steep place to be drowned in the lake. The result was that 'the whole multitude of the country of the Gadarenes round about besought him to depart from them; for they were taken with great fear' *(Luke 8.37)*. For our purposes, the people of Gadara may fairly be placed in the category of 'atheists', because, while they were Jews, they had spurned and disregarded their religious responsibilities and privileges. Their heavy involvement with forbidden animals is evidence enough of this. When they found themselves exposed to a double manifestation of the power of God, a marvellous healing and a judgement, and also to religious instruction, they became desperate for this influence to leave them. Their consciences were being stirred, and so they wanted the Lord out of their sight and away from their coasts as soon as possible.

This is exactly the spirit of atheism. Should there ever be a pang of conscience, or any spiritual manifestations or evidence, the atheistic heart wants it out of sight and out of mind. It must be smothered with a flurry of intellectual diversions and excuses.

We note that in this case the Lord did not argue with the Gadarene community, but left them with an unanswerable *testimony*. Luke records: 'Now the man out of whom the devils were departed besought him that he might be with him: but Jesus sent him away, saying, Return to thine own house, and shew how great things God hath done unto thee. And he went his way, and published throughout the whole city how great things Jesus had done unto him' *(Luke 8.38-39)*.

The method of the Lord was to leave stationed in that region a convert with a great personal testimony. There he would stand as a living rebuke to unbelief, and as a reminder to all of how God alone can transform character. Our words about our own conversion, and about the spiritual experience of others, will have greater effect than the most sophisticated intellectual reasoning, in the case of atheistic unbelievers. Let us, then, place the greatest stress on spiritual facts and testimony, rather than an *excess* of indirect reasoning.

4. Exposing the cruelties and impotence of atheism

We are given a strong pointer to the stance we should take with atheists even in the conduct of our Saviour toward Pilate at the time of the crucifixion. Pilate, though shaken within himself, stuck defiantly to his unbelief in the proud and contemptuous words he directed at Christ, saying, 'Speakest thou not unto me? knowest thou not that I have power to crucify thee, and have power to release thee?' *(John 19.10.)* The Lord had not answered Pilate's previous question, 'Whence art thou?' But now he answered, saying, 'Thou couldest have no power at all against me, except it were given thee from above.'

The lesson is that the atheist is a sinner in the hands of the mighty God, and he must not be encouraged to take the 'superior ground' of a sophisticated, superior thinker, standing in judgement upon Almighty God and his Truth. He must not be given the opportunity to dictate the agenda and dominate the discussion, conducting it as a lofty, condescending inspection of all the perceived weaknesses of God's case against him. We must not buckle to his line of reasoning, giving him licence to slander the Holy One, denigrate his purposes, ridicule the work of the Spirit, and pour contempt upon the Lord's people. We should not give him scope to buttress his wicked unbelief with an imagined victory over us.

Our assignment, by the help of the Spirit, is to turn the haughty, inquisitorial judge into a humble, needy seeker after Truth and grace, and we cannot do that by flattering his corrupt intellect, and whimpering under his verbal indignities. We must try to put the atheist on the run, and attack the gaping holes in his ideas, and the catastrophic results of his moral policies.

We may point to the obvious impotence of atheism to lift up human nature. In Western society over the last half-century, as belief in God has declined, so the impotence of atheism to reform and improve lives has been manifested. We may point to the moral cruelties which are so prevalent where there is no fear of God, whether seen in selfishness, violent crime, sexual abuse, child abuse, or in marriage breakdown with all its self-consideration, and callous indifference to children. Atheism equals cruelty, and we should emphasise that. Atheism is behind this selfish, immoral society in which everyone looks out for himself.

5. Exposing the intellectual dishonesty of atheism

We may also confront the common dishonesty of atheism in promoting its alternative morality. This is usually presented through fiction, rather than by argument, the entertainment industry brainwashing the public with movies and novels featuring nice, reasonable atheists, and narrow, miserable, bigoted religionists. Adultery, divorce, remarriage and LGBT relationships are constantly shown to be the reasonable and inevitable experiences of good people, while those who would disapprove are unreasonable and hypocritical. Through fiction, an atheistic Utopia is projected to the people. By ludicrous lies all find sensual satisfaction without penalty.

We may also challenge the unreasonableness of atheism. To quote Bridges, 'Let them be pressed with their own difficulties – far greater than those of the Gospel.' Why, for example, do evolutionists make no attempt to respond to the major objections of contrary voices in the scientific world? Why are the seemingly insurmountable problems about evolution never discussed, and objectors frequently dismissed from their university posts. Why do the priests of the evolutionary 'faith' behave in such a grossly unscientific and cowardly manner?

The answer is that militantly atheistic evolutionists are unreasonable people who *must* keep the 'faith', because not to do so would sweep away a vital foundation of atheism. Their evolutionary belief is itself a faith of the worst kind, maintained in the face of facts which challenge it, and energised by 'violent' prejudice.

We must challenge the atheist about his inability to account for the universe, for life, for the distinction between the human race and the animals, for the obvious evidence of design and complexity in the universe, for human moral consciousness and the faculty of reason, for the instinct for God, for the depravity of man, for the fact of reformation by spiritual conversion, and so on. Atheists have no explanation for any of these things.

6. Emphasising the immortality of the soul

We are given an example of how to deal with convinced atheists by the apostle Paul, addressing them on Mars' Hill *(Acts 17)*. There he faced Epicurean and Stoic philosophers who, after some discussion, had invited him to address the Areopagus, the supreme council of Athens, which regulated the city's religious and educational affairs. Gathered with the elders of Athens (for it was probably an informal session) was a 'public gallery' of interested Athenians and foreigners. Though Paul directed his message to all the outlooks represented, he particularly had in mind the Epicureans and Stoics who arranged the meeting. Not that they wanted to learn, but rather to indulge their patronising and scornful curiosity.

These people corresponded in several respects to present-day atheists. Epicureans believed that the chief end of life was happiness, and Stoics were rationalists. They did not believe in the immortality of the soul in a personal, continuing way. Paul's strategy for these philosophers was masterly. He began by speaking against idolatry in a manner which immediately grasped their attention, surprising them by advancing arguments similar to their own. They ridiculed idolaters for worshipping gods made by human hands. When they heard Paul saying exactly that, their respect was aroused. He used the element of surprise so often employed by the Saviour, then began to teach the lofty concept of one spiritual and yet personal God. Then he moved to the subject of personal conversion, and the fact of a coming day of judgement, no doubt including the atonement as he spoke of the resurrection.

Today atheists sneer at the Christian faith because they see the absurd distortions of nominal, unbiblical Christianity. They observe the insincerity and confusion so evident in much of the apostate Anglican church. Sometimes, it does not hurt to agree with the atheist, and so surprise him. We can agree with his condemnation of the lifeless variety of religion. We aim to show, as the apostle did, that the true religion is altogether different.

In *1 Corinthians 15.32* Paul condemns the motto of atheism, 'Let us eat and drink; for to morrow we die.' 'What point is there,' they say, 'in worrying about God or morals, if there is no afterlife? Let us do what we like, for when death comes, that will be the end!'

In seeking to stir the concern of atheists we remember what the preachers of long ago said about their viewpoint, pointing out that atheists are the greatest gamblers. Their entire outlook, lifestyle and policy depends on the assumption that there is no God and no soul, and that death is truly the end. But what if they are wrong? In all witness we must persistently chip away at this assumption, for it is their weakest and most vulnerable point, and their constitutional instinct for God and eternity is still alive within them. We must speak of eternity, of the coming day, and of the reality of Heaven and hell, because for many an atheist this will be the challenge causing greatest unease. Remember, to the atheist, everything is material and has come about by sheer chance. There is no Designer, no Creator, no ultimate purpose and no eternity. Our most challenging words will come when we speak of our eternal hope, and stress the reality of our experience of God's power and blessing.

In his ministry to 'atheistic' philosophers on Mars' Hill Paul emphasised the authority and sovereignty of God, who has fixed the lifespan of every human soul. He stressed the personal character of God, who must be sought by men and women, and who may be found and known. He spoke of the need for repentance, of the coming day of judgement, and of the resurrection and afterlife. These are the vital themes even for the most extreme atheists.

9
Prepared for Questions

ANSWERING QUESTIONS is the substance of personal witness, and the believer must be prepared for them. If we do not know how to respond to typical questions we will stumble at the finest opportunities. Biblical exhortations to witness warn that we must be ready for questions. Peter tells us to 'be ready always to give an answer to every man that asketh you a reason of the hope that is in you.' Paul says: 'Let your speech be alway with grace . . . that ye may know how ye ought to answer every man.'

The Lord's way of dealing with questions is the model for us. He did not necessarily give the kind of answer which his questioners expected, but neither did he avoid the question. He always gave the *spiritual* answer, and thus provided light on the way of salvation. People asked him many questions, some of these being only in their minds or murmured amongst themselves, but he knew their thoughts, and answered them. The Jewish leaders also asked questions, usually to trap him and make him appear heretical (from their point of view) or foolish. We also hear many hostile and defensive questions, and we must learn how to turn them to account so that we may minister the Gospel to the souls of our questioners.

By way of general observations, we observe that the Lord never answered at great length, and neither should we. Too much talking is the ruin of witness. The writer remembers the excitement of a lady who went out visiting homes in her neighbourhood, knocking on doors and telling people about the Lord. In a single week she gained admission into two flats in the same block, and spent a couple of hours in each presenting the Gospel, and answering questions at great length. The following week, to her distress, no one in that entire block would answer their door, although she knew the people were in. A long answer to a question outstays our welcome, and future witness is imperilled. Like the Lord, we must be self-disciplined and fairly brief. Remember also that the Lord's longest answers were in the interesting form of parables or illustrations.

But what is a 'spiritual' answer to a question? It is an answer which provides a *spiritual* explanation for the problem. Take, for example, the question asked by the Jews in the Nazareth synagogue at the time that the Lord began his ministry. They wondered at his 'gracious words', but they were perplexed and offended that a carpenter should teach in such a way, and they said, 'Is not this Joseph's son?' The simple answer would have been, 'Yes.' A longer answer might have explained that he was not strictly Joseph's son, but certainly Mary's, and proceeded to explain why their Messiah had entered the world through a humble family. The *spiritual* answer in this case was to show why the question had been asked, and to expose the prejudice which lay behind it. 'I tell you of a truth,' said the Lord, 'many widows were in Israel in the days of Elias . . . when great famine was throughout all the land; but unto none of them was Elias sent, save unto Sarepta, a city of Sidon, unto a woman that was a widow.'

The Lord also told them how only Naaman the Syrian was healed, and not any of the Jewish lepers in Israel in the days of Elisha. The problem laid bare was that prejudice and unbelief among the Jews had cut off the blessing of God before, and it had gone to Gentiles. The Lord laid his finger on their unbelief, and challenged their hearts.

When the scribes and Pharisees criticised the conduct of the Lord's disciples, saying, 'Why do ye eat and drink with publicans and sinners?' Christ answered in terms of his spiritual mission. 'I came not to call the righteous, but sinners to repentance.' At another time, when they demanded to know precisely when the kingdom of God would come, he replied in terms of the *spiritual* kingdom of God ruling in hearts, saying, 'The kingdom of God cometh not with observation . . . for, behold, the kingdom of God is within you.' The implication was that not all Jews were members of this kingdom, but only those who had God truly in their hearts.

The chief priest and the scribes, seeking to accuse him of treason, slyly asked, 'Is it lawful for us to give tribute unto Caesar, or no?' And he replied by showing the difference between earthly duties and heavenly duties. In the case of the woman taken in adultery the rulers said, 'Moses in the law commanded us, that such should be stoned: but what sayest thou?' And the Lord answered in such a manner that their own consciences were stirred, and their sin condemned.

Questions, therefore, are the most wonderful opportunities to give spiritual explanations. Even though the purpose of the questioner may be to confuse the issue, create a diversion, or even to scoff, we may be able to make a spiritual response and application. To train for this it is a good idea to write down all the questions which are heard repeatedly, and set ourselves the task of preparing good answers for future use. Where churches organise regular neighbourhood visitation, it is helpful for younger believers to be teamed up with experienced visitors so that they may learn how they deal with the questions.

A number of key questions, with answers, have been assembled by the author and are available as short videos; these may prove helpful for sharing with unconverted friends, and also for suggesting answers to those engaged in witness.* The answers provided are derived from ten-minute talks broadcast many years ago. Here are some of the questions:–

Why does God allow wars, sickness and tragedies? The answer, among other things, explains human rebellion, and speaks of how the human race has fouled up its world, cut itself off from God, become God's bitter enemy, and forfeited his help.

How can I be sure there is a God? The answer ranges briefly across the evidence of design and complexity, together with the strange condition of human beings, possessing the power of reason and moral conscience, coupled with hopeless weakness and tendency to failure. It is shown that only the biblical explanation accounts for such things. The answer also points out that the ultimate proof of God is available only to those who seek and find him.

The offensive type of question is also included, such as – *How can we be expected to take Christianity seriously? It is so narrow. You have to be so naive about life.* Here is a kind of protest question which needs to be courteously but firmly turned round to show that the non-Christian is the narrow and naive person, cut off from divine resources.

Why are there so many religions? To be asked such a question is a gift to the regular witnesser, who will point to the instinct for God which leads people to be religious, and also exposes their motives in inventing religions of their own, rather than accepting the true faith. It is an opportunity to explain why a *revealed* religion is so essential, and that only such a message could be authentic.

How can a God of love send people to hell? The answer is all Gospel, as the holiness and justice of God are explained, together with the necessity of forgiveness and new life. Human unbelief and

---

* https://www.metropolitantabernacle.org/Interested-in-the-Christian-Faith

rebellion is shown to be a vote against God and Heaven, which will be 'honoured' by God in the last day.

Is not religion just for the inadequate and dependent personality? This is a question representative of the proud and contemptuous type, and it is best answered by a portrayal of non-believing people as those who are *determined* to be restricted and limited in their lives. They opt for an incomplete existence, lacking spiritual knowledge and power, and living at the mercy of the material world.

These brief comments on the importance and usefulness of questions can barely touch the surface of the subject. An entire manual of suggested answers to different questions could usefully be compiled to help the ministry of personal witness.*

In answering questions our aim is to present the Lord, rather than to become entangled with the details of each question. It is important to remember that with the spiritual ignorance of the present day, people are often surprised to have very obvious matters explained. To emphasise in our answers that God is a *personal* God, and an approachable God, not an impersonal force, is most helpful to people. This is what their instincts tell them, but in an age when pantheistic ideas are all-pervasive, it is reassuring to have this stressed.

The manner in which questions are answered requires close personal monitoring. Some witnessing believers are inclined to get carried away, and to come across badly to their hearers. The text with which we began this chapter must be taken seriously. Peter says, 'But sanctify the Lord God in your hearts: and be ready always to give an answer to every man that asketh you a reason of the hope that is in you *with meekness and fear.*' This is a spiritual work. We are not defending our own opinions, but representing Almighty God.

---

* There are excellent books available to answer questions from people becoming involved in cults, such as the Jehovah's Witnesses and the Mormons – *JWs Answered Verse by Verse,* by David A. Reed, *Mormons Answered Verse by Verse,* by David A. Reed & John R. Farkas (published by Baker Book House, USA).

Our object is not to appear knowledgeable, or to win arguments, but to represent sincerely a perfect God and a saving message. Questions must be answered humbly, reverently, helpfully and courteously. They must be answered in full awareness of the possibility that God the Holy Spirit could well use our answers in the course of his regenerating, converting work in a soul.

Certainly we would not want the smallest trace of arrogance, haughtiness, overconfidence, impatience or peevishness to taint or ruin our answers in the estimation of our questioner, and our prayers and efforts will be directed to ensure that this shall never be so.

We conclude this glance at the need to prepare for questions with a comment on the way to send souls to Christ the Saviour. The chief end of all witness, including the answering of questions, is to urge lost people to go to Christ in prayer, and to seek his salvation. It is true that not every opportunity for witness, or every question answered, affords an appropriate moment for us to give our hearer a personal exhortation to seek the Lord. Naturally, we must be wise about this. On some occasions, it may be more appropriate to express the need to seek the Lord in a general rather than personal way. We may, for instance, say, 'Those who seek the Lord will be blessed,' rather than, 'You must seek the Lord, or you will be eternally lost.'

Some readers may have picked up Arminian phraseology, so that they find themselves wanting to say, 'You must receive Christ into your life.' This kind of expression is not only likely to confuse people, but it makes witness more difficult. It is much more natural, more understandable, and, of course, more biblical to bring the witness to conclusion with an exhortation along these lines – 'If you sincerely ask the Saviour for forgiveness and new life, you will receive it.' The biblical rule is that needy souls must be directed to apply to him; to go to him.

The Lord himself said, 'Come unto me!' He did not say to sinners,

'Ask me to come to you. Ask me into your lives.' Never forget the direction of the Lord's own exhortation to salvation in *Luke 11.9-10*. It is Godward! 'And I say unto you, Ask, and it shall be given you; seek, and ye shall find; knock, and it shall be opened unto you. For every one that asketh receiveth; and he that seeketh findeth; and to him that knocketh it shall be opened.' The direction is important. We send people to him, and as we do so we pray for them, that God will overrule in their hearts, and that they will trust him, and go to him.

The Lord has ordained the ministry of personal witness, and he will not let us go on in the work unblessed. In the giving of the great commission, our ever faithful Lord said, 'Lo, I am with you alway, even unto the end of the world.' He gave his people also the great promise of fruitfulness, saying, 'Ye have not chosen me, but I have chosen you, and ordained you, that ye should go and bring forth fruit, and that your fruit should remain' *(John 15.16)*. The Lord will certainly bless his loyal servants, and strengthen and encourage, until the day they hear his matchless voice saying, 'Well done, thou good and faithful servant: thou hast been faithful over a few things . . . enter thou into the joy of thy lord' *(Matthew 25.21)*.

Evangelistic Publications by Dr Peter Masters
(all available through the Wakeman Trust)

A5-size evangelistic booklets:

How to Seek and Find the Lord
Intended for seekers, the author emphasises that there is only one way of salvation, clearly defined and revealed by God in his Word. He then explains the kind of belief and attitude which brings a seeker to find the Lord.

Vanity of Vanities
Subtitled *The Emptiness of Life Without God*. This booklet presents the experience of King Solomon, who experimented with every conceivable kind of pleasure, and concluded that life is pointless and predictable, unless people seek and find the Lord God, and know his power and guidance in their lives.

The Rebellious Years
Subtitled *The Need for Self-Understanding*. This booklet is intended to help readers from mid-teenage to late twenties to understand the source of the inner rebellion that urges us all away from God in the 'second quarter' of life.

What You Should Know About Your Conscience
What is the mysterious faculty of conscience, and how does it function? What happens when it is abused, or attempts are made to reprogramme it? Points to the only way of 'purging' the conscience.

A Seeker's Problems
Often when people are convinced of the need for conversion to Christ they experience difficulty in seeking and finding him as Saviour. This booklet answers ten problems encountered by serious seekers. These are not questions

or doubts about the faith, but personal hindrances in approaching Christ, by faith. Many seekers have been helped by the advice given here.

A booklet for those who witness:

Seven Certain Signs of True Conversion

Dr Masters here lists the biblical indications that a person has been truly converted, so that those who witness for Christ and help seekers may know how to give correct counsel and advice. Examples of right and wrong counsel are provided.

Books to help in evangelism:

Men of Destiny and *Men of Purpose* are two very popular volumes of Christian biography, presenting the lives and conversion experiences of 25 famous, unusual or even notorious people, including royals, Reformers, and 'fathers' of modern science.

Given to unconverted people, these books challenge the heart and open the way to further spiritual influence. For the preacher, youth leader, or Sunday School teacher, they provide outstanding testimonies to illustrate and enrich messages for years to come.

Men of Destiny

166 pages, paperback, Wakeman Trust, ISBN 978 1 870855 55 6

Tsar Alexander Pavlovich *(The tsar who defeated Napoleon)*
Lieut 'Birdie' Bowers *(Scott's 'bravest man' in the Antarctic)*
Sir James Simpson *(The discoverer of anaesthetic chloroform)*
Alves Reis *(The counterfeiter who nearly owned his country)*
Joshua Poole *(The story of 'Fiddler Joss', drunkard turned preacher)*
Viscount Alexander of Hillsborough *(A leader of the House of Lords)*
John Newton *(The transformed slave-trader)*
Jean Henri Dunant *(Founder of the International Red Cross)*
Martin Luther *(The ex-monk who led the Reformation)*
Bilney, Tyndale & Latimer *(Three heroic English martyrs)*
Alfred the Great *(The king who organised England)*
Lieut-General Sir William Dobbie *(World War II hero of Malta)*

Men of Purpose
157 pages, paperback, Wakeman Trust, ISBN 978 1 870855 41 9

Michael Faraday *(Father of electrical science)*
Henry J. Heinz *(Founder of the food empire)*
Felix Mendelssohn *(A composer with a spiritual journey)*
Lord Radstock *(Whose missions brought conversions to Russia's aristocracy)*
James Clerk Maxwell *(Father of modern physics)*
Philip P. Bliss *(The hymnwriter who won countless souls)*
Fred Charrington *(The brewer who renounced a fortune)*
Lord Kelvin *(Britain's greatest scientific inventor)*
James Montgomery *(A poet who ran away from God)*
Sir John Ambrose Fleming *(Inventor of the radio valve)*
Daniel Defoe *(The founder of journalism and great novelist)*